BLOG(

M000028093

My
Blogging
Secrets

BY AMBER McNAUGHT

CONTENTS

forever amber

1

THE ONLY BLOGGING SECRET
YOU'LL EVER NEED TO KNOW

Hi, my name's Amber, and I'm a full-time blogger.

Yes, one of the ones who writes about her life and gets paid for it. I know, weird, right? I mean, who would seriously pay someone just to write about themselves, and all of the totally unremarkable things they get up to every day? More importantly, who would read it? No one, surely. Or not enough people to make it a viable business, anyway. People might say that blogging is their "job", but everyone knows it's not a real job, right? Right?

Wrong, actually. Blogging is my full-time job, and sole source of income, and it currently earns me more than I was making in my last "real" job (local government PR, in case you're interested: I wasn't interested, unfortunately, which is one of the reasons I ended up as a blogger...), and way more than I made in my first "real" job, as a newspaper journalist. Blogging pays the bills, keeps me in shoes, and, two years ago, allowed me to buy a new house, which I'm currently in the process of renovating - a process which is also being partly funded by my blog.

To be fair, I don't just write about my life. I also take photos of my outfits... which is even more strange when it comes to occupations you get paid for, now I come to think of it. I don't just have one blog, either: at the time of writing, I have three, and I used to have even more than that. I'm gradually attempting to downsize, though, and I firmly believe that one blog is all you need in order to make a decent living, so that one blog is the one I'll be concentrating on in this book. Think of it as the one blog to rule them all, if you will. Or just as 'Forever Amber' if you prefer, because, well, that's its name. (ForeverAmber.co.uk, if you want its full title.)

Of course, if you read my blog (and chances are you've at least glanced at it, if you bought this book), you already know all of this. What you want to know is how I did it. How did I go from being a stressed-out office worker heading for a nervous breakdown, to someone who didn't get out of bed until 9am this morning, and will spend her day taking photos of her shoes, and calling it "work" - oh, and getting paid for it, into the bargain?

Well, you're in luck, because this book will tell you all of my blogging "secrets". Before you read any further, it's important that you understand what this book is not. It's not a step-by-step guide to how to start up a blog, for one thing. I'm not to walk you through the process of purchasing a domain, or metaphorically hold your hand while you set up a blog, and figure out how to post your first article. I'm going to trust that you're clever enough to be able to do all of that already - or to be able to Google it all, at least.

This is also not a definitive guide to making money from blogging: one of the greatest things about this brand-new industry is that it's constantly evolving, and if I were to attempt to list every single way you could potentially turn your blog into a business, then a) I'd be here forever and b) the information would be out of date by the time I'd finished typing it. These are simply MY secrets: the techniques I've used personally, and the things I feel have been instrumental in helping me turn my blog into a career.

By telling you how I did it, I'm hoping to give you some insight into how to to take that blog you've just created, and turn it into a profitable business: one which will - eventually - earn you enough to live off. (The word "eventually" is key to that sentence, by the way. Don't say I didn't warn you...) And with all of that said, I'm sure I'm probably breaking some golden rule of ebook-writing here by telling you this upfront, but I'm going to start off by revealing the biggest blogging "secret" of all. It's this:

THERE ARE NO "SECRETS" TO BECOMING A SUCCESSFUL BLOGGER.

In other words, the secret is that there isn't one. End of book. Let's all go home early!

I'm being totally serious here, by the way: I wrote this book because when people find out I blog for a living, they almost immediately ask me what my "secret" is. How did I get my blog to the point where it was getting over 180,000 pageviews per month? How do I make enough money to survive? How can they do it too?

Whenever I'm asked these questions, I'm always left with the impression that what the person is really looking for is some kind of easy answer - a magic formula, whereby I'll be able to tell them, "Well, if you do this, then you'll get 10,000 followers overnight," or "There's this website you go to, and if you type in the name of your blog, it sends you 50,000 visitors a day!" They want me to tell them it's easy, in other words: or easy if you just know HOW. Here's the thing, though:

It isn't easy.

Oh, I know blogging LOOKS easy. Of course it does. Bloggers post constant photos of themselves out buying peonies in the middle of the day, before stopping for a hard-earned Starbucks break, and the people who follow them think that's all there is to it. It just doesn't GET much easier than that, does it?

But blogging isn't "easy", and there are no magic secrets to success. In some cases, you might NEVER really know what it was that made a particular blogger successful, because here's another not-so-secret secret:

Sometimes it just comes down to sheer, dumb luck.

Many of the biggest bloggers out there, for instance, got where they are now simply by being in the right place at the right time. They either got in early, and rode the wave, or they lucked out and just so happened to have a great story, or a post that went viral, or even just really great hair. (And no, I'm not joking. Never underestimate the power of really good hair...)

As for the rest of us, though? The rest of us got where WE are (which probably isn't even CLOSE to where those super-famous bloggers are, by the way...) through hard work and a lot of patience. And that's really all there is to it.

If you're already feeling short-changed, and wondering why you bought this book if all I'm going to tell you is to work hard and keep at it, don't. I AM going to share the "secrets" of my blogging success with you, and I hope at least some of them will help you understand what it takes to build a successful blog. I want you to be realistic about it, though. I don't want you to read this thinking it's some kind of "get rich quick" scheme: or even that you're going to get "rich". Most of all, I want you to understand that "success" is a relative term. In my case, for instance, "success" means getting paid to do something I'm truly passionate about: something I love so much it doesn't actually feel like work to me. Success means waking up every morning and knowing I'm free to set my own schedule, write about whatever I want, and still know I'm going to be able to pay my bills this month, and maybe even have a little left over for those awesome shoes I saw last week.

It's not the kind of success that sees me swanning around St. Tropez in designer clothes, on an all-expenses-paid vacation, or hiring a private jet to transport me and all my monogrammed luggage around the world in style. I mean, I'd love it if it WAS, but I'm not that kind of blogger, and the fact is, most of us aren't. Can I get a tiny violin over here, please?

I started this on a bit of a downer, didn't I? Let's redress the balance slightly, then, by acknowledging that while successful blogging might take a lot of work, it'll (hopefully) be some of the rewarding work you'll ever do in your life. Which brings me to my next big "secret"...

AMBER McNAUGHT

2

THE MAIN REASON MY
BLOG BECAME SUCCESSFUL

WHY IT HELPS TO HATE YOUR JOB

If you want to be a full-time blogger, it helps to hate your existing job. Like, really, really hate it. So much that you stand crying in the shower every morning at the thought of heading into the office, and try to kiss people with the flu, in the hope that you'll catch it and get a few days off. Because lying in bed surrounded by Lemsip and used tissues is about a hundred times better that going to work, right? It was for me, anyway, and that, in a nutshell, is the secret of my success. (No, that doesn't mean you can stop reading, I'm afraid: I'm just getting started here...)

Why am I telling you to hate your job? Do I actually want you to be miserable?

Nope. I'm not that cruel. It helps to hate your existing job, because if you hate your existing job, you'll be prepared to do almost anything to escape it. This is good, because as a professional blogger, you'll have to do almost anything - and then a bit more.

The thing that most people don't understand about blogging is that it's hard . No, really, it is. It's not hard in the way working in a coal mine, or going into a war zone, is hard, granted. But it's hard in the way that starting a business from scratch, and then trying to turn it into a profit-making enterprise, which makes enough money to support you and your family, is hard. Because that's what it is. Blogging for money is starting a business from scratch and then trying to wring a profit from it, and that's the first thing you're going to have to understand before you go any further.

Blogging is a business. If you think it's "just a hobby", or that it should only ever be a hobby, you actually can stop reading now, because I'm not going to be able to help you - or not without a huge shift of attitude on your part.

A lot of people, you see, look at full-time bloggers, and they think it's going to be easy. They see the pretty pictures and the glossy lifestyles they portray, and they think, "Hey! These girls [Because they're almost always girls, aren't they, these professional bloggers, with their Starbucks cups and their marble backdrops which are just SO perfect on Instagram!] are getting paid to wear clothes and go about their lives! All they have to do is take a few quick pictures and hit the 'publish' button, and they're laughing all the way to the nearest branch of Nordies, to stock up on more clothes. I'll have some of that, then!"

If that's what you think full-time blogging is going to be like, I want you to pack up your things and go home. No, seriously: you're dreaming. You're confusing the end product with what it took to create it. And what it takes to create the kind of blog that actually makes money - any money at all, much less the money you'll need just to survive every month - is a whole lot more than that. The fact is, those girls aren't just getting paid to wear clothes and go about their lives. No one gets paid just to live their life, trust me. Not even the Kardashians, or the Royal Family.

What they're getting paid for, you see, is to sell you the clothes they're wearing, the makeup they're reviewing, the product they're showing you. They're not paid to eat in nice restaurants - they're paid to convince you to go to that restaurant and spend your hard-earned cash in it.

Do you see how different that is from simply going about your life and getting paid for it? In order to persuade you that the thing they're selling is good enough for you to spend money on it, the blogger has to present it in a way that makes it look really, really good: a way that makes you look at that dress, or lipstick, or whatever it is, and think, "I must have that, and I must have it now! In fact, I'm going to click on this link right here and buy it instantly!"

If you think, "That's nice, but I'm going to think about it for a while, maybe buy it in a few weeks, when I have some spare cash," or even, "I like it, but I'm going to go to the store and try it on, first," the blogger makes nothing. So she has to be good enough to make you read her blog post and immediately take action - and getting that good takes time, effort and a whole lot of work. If it didn't... well, you wouldn't need this book, would you? You'd already be sitting in the first-class compartment, jetting off to some sun-drenched island, to spend all that easy money you made from your blog.

You're not, though. And I'm not either, actually, because here's the other thing you need to understand about full-time blogging: hardly any of us get "rich" from it. Oh, there are plenty of us making a living from it, sure: but making a living is very different from making a fortune, so if you've been looking at the really big bloggers - the ones who're rumoured to be making millions of dollars every year, and who swan around in designer clothes, at a different vacation spot every month - and thinking that'll be you this time next year, again, I'm sorry to be the one to break it to you, but it probably won't. Sorry. I mean, it could be you, of course. Anything is possible, after all, and someone has to make the big bucks, right?

Most of the "big" bloggers, however, got where they are through a combination of hard work, talent, luck, and simply being in the right place at the right time. You can achieve the first of those, and you might even have the second, but you can't bank on the last two, so while I don't want to stamp on anyone's dreams here, and I do genuinely believe that anything is possible in this wonderful world of blogging, I'm going to keep on reminding you to be realistic about it.

(And seeing as I'm in the mood for dashing people's hopes, there's no Easter Bunny, either. Sorry.)

I'm also going to tell you again that it helps if you hate your job. I did, and that's the main secret to my blogging success. If I hadn't hated my job as much as I did, I probably wouldn't be where I am now. In fact, I know I wouldn't, because the thing is, I'd dreamt of starting a business for years before I took the plunge, and I'd never been brave enough to actually do it.

Because it requires a touch of bravery, too, blogging. Not the "running into a burning building to save a trapped kitten" kind of bravery, you understand - I'm not trying to say bloggers are the real-life heroes of our time or anything like that. But the kind of bravery that makes you quit your job without having anything else to go to, knowing that whatever money you make from here on out will be completely down to you, and your ability to type words on a screen that will resonate enough with people that they'll want to follow you, read your posts, click on your links. The kind of bravery that allows you to live without knowing where the next paycheck is coming from, and trust that it WILL come from somewhere - you just have to work out where, and then make it happen.

It's not the same kind of bravery that we're used to associating with that word, true. (It's more like the kind of bravery that let's you wear two clashing prints together, or turn up in heels on Casual Friday), but it does require a leap of faith. Mostly, though, it requires a lot of determination. You have to really, really want it. Enough that you'll be willing to work round the clock, sacrifice your holidays and weekends for it, and basically make your blog business the centre of your life for as long at it takes to get it to turn a profit: and for a long time after that too, if I'm honest.

The main reason my blog became successful was that I absolutely hated my job - and hating my job was making me hate my life, too. Because I hated my job, I was willing to do whatever it took to escape it - I didn't really care how. I was willing to work hard, take a huge pay cut, and live with the uncertainty that comes with self-employment, and the reason I was willing to do it was because the alternative (either staying in a job I hated, or getting another one I knew I'd hate every bit as much) was so unthinkable to me.

You don't really have to hate your job, then. But you do have to be able to find that motivation from somewhere, so before you decide to turn your blog into a business, I want you to sit down, get yourself a pen and paper - or an iPhone, or laptop, or whatever you like to write on - and write down your motivation. Do it now, before you go any further. Understanding your motivation is the key to knowing if you have what it takes to be a successful blogger, and it will also help you work out just how you're going to go about achieving that aim. Here's mine...

HOW I QUIT MY JOB TO START A BLOG

When I decided I wanted to start my own business, I was in my second job after university, and the unhappiest I'd ever been in my life.

My first job had been in journalism - I was the chief reporter for a local paper (That might sound impressive, but when I tell you that for a long time I was also the ONLY reporter, you'll probably revise your opinion of that...) and I liked it, but knew I would probably never progress beyond the level I was at - and that I didn't really want to, either.

I was getting paid to write, sure: that was, after all, the reason I'd gotten into journalism in the first place - writing was my passion in life, and it was the only thing I'd ever really known how to do. So now I was writing, and I was getting paid for it, but I wasn't writing about the things I wanted to write about. Instead, I was writing about the goings-on of the local community: the planning disputes, the council meetings, the golden weddings and local gala days.

There's absolutely nothing wrong with any of that, of course - they're worthy stories, and they need to be told. They weren't, however, the kind of stories I wanted to tell. They weren't the kind of stories that had me jumping out of bed in the middle of the night, scrambling for a pen and paper so I could get that idea down. They weren't the kind of stories that make people come up to me and say, "You know, that story really resonated with me..."

So, I wanted to write, and that was my first motivation.

I also, however, knew I wanted to write about... well, the things I wanted to write about , rather than the things I was told to write about, which, more often than not, held absolutely no interest for me whatsoever. What I wanted to write about, though, wasn't exactly the kind of thing anyone was going to offer to pay me for in a hurry. I'd discovered by this point, you see, that what I most enjoyed writing about - and there's no way to say this without sounding horribly self-absorbed, so apologies for that - was myself. I think I just threw up a little bit in my mouth as I typed that.

I knew I wasn't a journalist: I was good at writing the stories, but I wasn't good at going out and finding them, which is a huge part of the job. One day a colleague of mine from our sister evening paper was sent on a "death knock" - knocking on the door of a couple whose child had just died in a horrible accident, and asking to interview them. I knew nothing would ever persuade me to do that: I just didn't have it in me, and that, combined with my terminal shyness, meant my career in newspaper journalism was always going to be short-lived.

I knew I wasn't a fiction writer, either. I'd tried - oh, how I'd tried - to write novels, short stories, poems - anything at all that could be described as "creative" writing, and, again, I just couldn't do it. If someone told me the story, I could do a pretty good job of writing it, but I couldn't make stuff up, and, more importantly (for me), I didn't particularly enjoy it.

That left me with personal writing: the kind of thing I'd been doing in my diaries for years, and had recently transitioned to doing on Livejournal, which was basically an early blogging community. I loved writing the little anecdotes from my day-to-day life: I enjoyed recording the minutiae of my days, or just ranting about the things that were really important to me. The problem is, though, that people don't generally pay for that kind of writing. "WANTED: Girl to write about her life, and which pair of shoes she decided to wear this morning" - said no job advert ever.

It was a bit of a bind, really.

After two years in journalism, however, I was laid off, and got a new job - this time working in local government PR. I was still writing for a living, but now I was writing press releases and annual reports, along with articles for the website.

I hated every minute of it.

Like, crying-in-the-shower level hate.

I was bored, for one thing. I always did the job to the best of my ability, but I had absolutely zero interest in the things I was writing about, so I really struggled to remain motivated - and sometimes just to remain awake.

Most of all, though, I felt trapped. Every day I'd get up and drive to that office, knowing that I wouldn't be allowed to leave it for eight whole hours: eight hours which passed so slowly I was always amazed not to have aged by the time I left every evening. Eight hours during which my time was not my own: it literally belonged to someone else, and all of the things that made me happy, or at least just made life bearable, were absolutely forbidden to me.

I couldn't talk to my fiancé.

I couldn't talk to my friends.

I spent more time with my colleagues than I did with my family, and although my colleagues were perfectly nice people, I had nothing in common with them other than work - which made things kinda awkward when my boss started insisting on compulsory "team-building" activities, which soon saw my evenings and weekends being taken over, too.

Now I didn't even have free time to myself, and the little time I did have was spent catching up with all of the housework and chores I couldn't do during the week, when I was at work. I was absolutely miserable, and could see little point to a life in which every waking second was monopolised by a job I hated: all except for maybe two weeks holiday per year, the first of which I'd spend sleeping, exhausted by my own misery, and the second I'd spend dreading coming home. Not that holidays were a problem I was likely to be having for a long time, though, because, towards the end of my second year in PR, my fiancé was diagnosed with end-stage renal failure, and told that, unless he started dialysis immediately, he had around two weeks to live.

Which kinda put a damper on things, to be honest.

We'd gotten engaged one week before his diagnosis, in a romantic scene on the banks of the Grand Canyon - a scene which totally belied the fact that Terry hadn't slept for a week at that point, and had spent the entire year getting gradually more and more ill, with a condition which his doctor diagnosed as a bad case of acid reflux, but which turned out to be complete renal failure. We don't use that doctor any more, needless to say.

It would be wrong of me to present Terry's illness (and subsequent treatment: he had a successful transplant two years later, almost to the day, receiving a kidney donated by his brother, John. That's another spoiler for you there, but I couldn't have you thinking this was going to be a sad story, could I?) as a "come to Jesus" moment, because it was only afterwards that it started to feel that way. At the time, you just get through it as best you can.

I remember during those two years of dialysis, and all of the horrors they were filled with, people would frequently tell me how "brave" we were both being, but I didn't feel brave at all: I just didn't have a choice. It wasn't like someone came to us, and said, "Look, you can either have kidney failure or you can not have it: now what's it gonna be?" (If they had, we'd have picked "NOT kidney failure", because, screw "bravery", seriously...) I did have a choice about work, though, and when all of your other choices are taken away from you, you want to grab the ones that are left with both hands. So while there was no lightbulb moment when I suddenly thought, "Life's too short to spend it doing something you hate," I did come to realise that, well, life is too short to spend it doing something you hate. And that's what I'd been doing.

Every day I'd sit at my desk and look out of the office window at the world passing by - something I took quite literally. The world was actually passing me by, I thought. I had no real place in it: all of those people out there walking around in the sunshine (or, OK, the rain): they had a life. All I had was a job, and I'd come to see the two as being mutually exclusive. For as long as I was forced to remain stuck in this job (Or any job, really, because I'd learned enough about myself by this point to know that it wasn't the job that was the problem: it was ME.) I'd feel trapped - and feeling trapped was slowly but surely destroying my life.

As corny as it sounds, I wanted to be free, and that was my second motivation. I was prepared to do anything necessary to just not feel the way I felt any more. I was prepared to give up my decent salary, and all of the security that came with having a "good" job, because I knew by now that money and security were not my main motivations. Freedom was. (It's OK to cringe at that statement, by the way: I certainly cringed while I was writing it...)

When you hate your job or life, a lot of people will try to tell you that it's all about your attitude, and that you "just have to be positive", to "turn that frown upside down!" and all of that kind of inspirational-Facebook-status stuff. They'll tell you to change your approach, and learn to love the life you have, rather than pining for the one you want.

I'm not going to tell you any of that, though.

Because I didn't try to change my attitude, or learn to love the life I had. Instead, I quit my job and started a blog.

Well, somebody had to. Right?

AMBER McNAUGHT

3

HOW I CREATED A BLOG
THAT BECAME A BUSINESS

SOME THINGS I DIDN'T DO BEFORE QUITTING MY JOB, BUT WHICH YOU PROBABLY SHOULD

Whoa, there, cowboy! Yeah, you there, with your resignation letter all typed up and ready to hand in, so you can go and start making money by posting photos of your lunch to Instagram every day: not so fast. The fact is, when I say I quit my job and started a blog, I'm telling the truth - but it wasn't like I just started making money from it right away. No, it was more like I quit my job, started a blog... then several years later I started to make just enough money to get by on.

I don't recommend this course of action.

No, seriously, DO NOT QUIT YOUR JOB in the belief that starting a blog will instantly replace your salary, because it won't. Not instantly, and maybe not ever, actually. (Well, not unless you read to the end of the book and follow all of my top tips, obviously. Ahem.)

My own decision wasn't so much a "decision" as it was something I was forced into through circumstances. My fiance was on dialysis three times a week, and would need a kidney transplant in order to survive. I was working in a job I hated, and felt like every good thing in my life had been replaced by stress, misery, and the endless monotony of spending my entire life feeling like I was on a treadmill I just couldn't get off. To say I was stressed was an understatement, and one fine day in April (I mean, I SAY it was a fine day - I was long past the stage of even noticing the weather by that stage), it all got to be too much for me, so I walked out of my office and never went back.

You'll gather from this that there's a lot I'm not saying here, and you're right: there is. No one's story is quite that simple, but as this is a true story, and because even bloggers like to keep some things to themselves (and also like to avoid being sued...), I'm going to skim over the details, and simply say that one day I got up and drove to work as usual, and the next day I didn't.

And that I don't recommend that for a second.

Here I some things I DIDN'T do before quitting my job to start blogging, but which I strongly recommend you at least consider:

1. Get your finances in order

The most important thing to realise about any form of self-employment is that it marks the beginning of years on end of financial uncertainty, and if you're used to the security of a guaranteed paycheck every month, that can be pretty hard to deal with. Because my, er, journey into self-employment was unplanned, I was woefully unprepared for this. I'd always been something of a spendthrift: the kind of person who lived paycheck-to-paycheck, and who, as soon as her salary hit her account, would run out and spend it all, leaving just enough to live off ramen noodles for the rest of the month - if that. Well, who needs food when you have great shoes, right?

Not even the mortgage payments on the new house Terry and I had bought almost exactly a year before his kidney failure diagnosis (great timing, huh?) had manged to temper my spending: basically, if I wanted it, and I had the money in my account for it, I'd buy it, without giving a thought to what else I should be doing with that money. What's the point of saving for a rainy day, after all, when every day is rainy? Life is for living, I'd tell myself, as I handed over my card in exchange for yet another pair of shoes: it wasn't like I had anything else in my life to enjoy, so if I was going to spend my days trapped in an office, and my evenings and weekends on a dialysis ward, without even the promise of a holiday (thrice-weekly dialysis sessions kinda put the brakes on your travel plans...), I was damn sure I'd be well-dressed while I did it.

Yeah, I was pretty stupid. And because I was pretty stupid, I started self-employment with not just a mortgage to cover, and all of the usual household expenses, but with a pile of credit card bills, a car loan, and bank statements I was too scared to open when they dropped through the door.

I had some really great shoes, though, so there was that.

In my defense, I didn't actually know I was about to become self-employed when I got myself into this mess. You do, which is why you're going to be much cleverer than I was, and you're going to sort out your finances before you even think about quitting your job. You don't have to be totally unrealistic about this, of course: I'm not suggesting that you need to pay off your mortgage before signing up for that Wordpress account, but I DO suggest that you clear as much debt as you can, so you can start with as clean a financial slate as possible. The last thing you want to be worrying about when you start your new blogging business is how you're going to pay the bills this month - trust me when I tell you there are more than enough things to worry about without adding more to the mix - so learn from my mistakes (Well, I feel like someone should learn from them, and it doesn't look like it's going to be me...), and get your finances in order.

I buy the shoes so you don't have to: remember that.

2. Set a budget

If you'd asked me before I started blogging exactly how much money I thought I needed to live off every month, I wouldn't have been able to answer you, because I just can't count that high. No matter how much I earned, I'd always be able to come up with something else I had to have, and right up to the point when my life changed overnight with Terry's diagnosis, I was convinced I couldn't possibly have lived on a penny less than I was making. I needed the high-end makeup I was buying. I had to have that new coat I'd seen in the sales. I couldn't possibly go to work in this old suit - I needed a new one, and I needed it now.

All of this is absolute rubbish, of course: I know that now. The fact is, I couldn't possibly have picked a worse time to quit my job. Terry had been in his job for just a couple of months when disaster struck: he couldn't work while he was on dialysis (Some days he'd feel OK, but other days the treatment would leave him feeling so faint and sick he could barely even stand up...), and although the company he worked for did their best to help him, the sick pay didn't last long, leaving us without an income. Obviously things had to change. With Terry concentrating on his health, and just getting through every day, I took control of the finances, and if you're thinking that sounds a bit like putting a toddler in charge of running the country, you'd be right. Harsh, but right.

I did it, though, and I did it by cutting out every single unnecessary expense. Holidays and evenings out were already off the cards, thanks to the dialysis, and soon everything else went, too. There were no more expensive beauty purchases for me: I switched from the high-end city salon I'd previously used to a local place around the corner, where they gave me a mullet I didn't ask for (does anyone actually ASK for a mullet?), but only charged me £10. After that, I just stopped having haircuts altogether: well, there's only so much a girl can take.

I whittled the household budget down, too, swapping the weekly supermarket blitz for near-daily trips to the budget versions, where I'd challenge myself to see how little I could spend without starving. I sold all of my office clothes on eBay, thinking I wouldn't need them again - then I sold pretty much the rest of my closet too, because money was money, and I needed money more than I needed dresses. (I still regret selling that beautiful tweed coat, though. God, that was a thing of beauty...) We didn't go out - not ever. I mean, we'd see friends and family, but there were no more meals in restaurants or trips to the cinema - we just couldn't afford it, so we didn't do it.

All of this might sound pretty dire, but actually, it wasn't as bad as you'd think. It wasn't even as bad as I'd think, because the thing I learned from all of this was that I didn't need nearly as much money to live on as I'd thought. I'm not saying I didn't miss my old lifestyle, because I definitely did - I'd frequently pause in front of shop windows and stare longingly at what was inside, hoping I looked like Audrey Hepburn in Breakfast at Tiffany's, but actually just looking a bit sad, standing in front of New Look, wearing the only pair of jeans I hadn't sold on eBay yet. But I digress. I'm going to say something really cheesy and obvious here, so I apologise in advance, but it has to be said...

Money isn't what brings you happiness.

It really isn't. Before Terry got ill, if someone had tried to say that to me, I'd have retorted that they obviously weren't shopping in the right places, but the reason my new, frugal lifestyle was easier than I'd have expected it to be was because of what I said in the last chapter: I'd discovered my motivation, and - here comes the cheese - had realised that what mattered most to me wasn't clothes and makeup and money, but having the freedom to live my life on my own terms, without constantly feeling trapped by my job. (And, of course, health. Because as we're always hearing, if you don't have your health, you don't have much. That one really IS true.)

(I'll stop with the clichés now, I promise.)

Well, we didn't have our health: Terry for obvious reasons, and me simply because the stress I'd been living with for the past few months had really taken its toll. But we now had some degree of freedom, and the ability to build on that, and make something of our lives - something that wouldn't leave me crying in the shower every morning at 6am, and staring out of the office window, feeling like life was passing me by.

It wasn't much, but it was a start. So before you start your blog business, sit down and work out a budget you can stick to. Make it realistic - you're going to be a blogger, not a monk -

but try to be honest with yourself about what you really need to make every month just to cover the basics. Above all, understand that when you first start out with your new venture, you're going to be poor: possibly for a long time. By working out what you can live on - and what you really can't live without - you'll give yourself a much better chance of getting through those lean times, and will also be better placed to know if full-time blogging really is the way to go.

And, I mean, it might not be. You might read all of the above, and think, "Screw that! I really can't live without my weekly manicures and weekend breaks in St. Tropez!" That's totally fine, by the way: blogging full-time might be a dream job to some, but it has the potential to be an absolute nightmare for others. At least now you'll know, right?

3. Save up enough money to cover your first few months

I've told you how bad I was (and still am, if I'm honest) with money, so it's pretty rich of me (no pun intended) to be telling you to start saving, isn't it? Needless to say, as with all of the other points on this list, I didn't save a penny before quitting my job. (Again, in my defense, I feel I have to reiterate that I didn't plan ANY of this. I like to think that if I'd known I'd be quitting my well-paid job to become a blogger, I'd have planned things out a lot more carefully, but then again, I also like to think I'm funny, and that I can totally pull off that bodycon dress I just bought, so maybe take that with a pinch of salt.)

Here's where the luck comes into my story, however, because not long after I left the office for the last time, Terry, who had been passing his time during those long dialysis sessions by messing around on a laptop, and teaching himself web design (He'd always built websites in his spare time, but had never thought about doing it professionally), managed, thanks to a few lucky connections, to land himself a freelance web design job.

Now, this would've been good news for us anyway, but when I found out how much the company in question were willing to pay Terry to build their website, I realised just how good this news was. I can still remember the day Terry called me from his dialysis chair to tell me his pitch had been successful: I was so excited I danced around the kitchen with the dog, then cleaned it from top to bottom. (The kitchen, not the dog. Er, I clean to work off energy, what of it?)

We knew this was an opportunity we couldn't afford to miss, and it opened up a whole world of possibility for us. That night we sat down and worked out what we'd do with this unexpected windfall, and agreed that, rather than spending it, or simply frittering it away, the most sensible thing to do would be to put it into a bank account and try not to touch it: to save it for that rainy day, in other words.

(Yeah, I know: it was already pouring. And I also said I'd stop spouting clichés. But you know what I mean.)

Now, don't get me wrong, it wasn't a huge amount of money. Given our new, super-frugal lifestyle, however, and my own newfound budgeting skills, I knew I could make that cheque stretch for several months - maybe even longer. If we were really careful, it would maybe take us to the end of the year, and wouldn't that be a relief?

Having some savings was good, however, but having even more savings would be even better, and it didn't take us long to realise that if one company had been willing to pay Terry to design a website for them, other companies might do the same. Moreover, people who need websites built generally also need content for those sites, so what if Terry designed the websites and I wrote the content? By doing that, we could offer an all-inclusive service, which would allow both of us to work from home, and hopefully earn enough to never have to go back to the jobs we'd hated.

By the end of the month, we'd registered a limited company (Hot Igloo Productions Ltd - a name suggested by my mum after a long, wine-fueled brainstorming session), opened a business bank account, and launched our own website.

None of this would've been possible without that initial windfall: an amount which I kept untouched for years, protecting it the way a mama bear protects her cubs. That money was our safety net: without it, we'd have been so busy worrying about where our next meal was coming from, and how we'd pay that bill (I used to literally lie awake at night worrying about what we'd do if the boiler broke down. I only ever got as far as "panic" before I'd put that into practice and start panicking for real), that we wouldn't have been able to start a business. Hell, until then, I'd been so busy worrying about money I'd barely been able to comb my own hair.

My final piece of advice to you, then, is to get yourself a safety net. And I know: you're probably reading this and thinking, "Well, that's all well and good, but that money essentially just landed in your lap, Amber: you didn't do anything to deserve it, and not everyone is going to be that lucky." You're totally right, of course: I got my safety net through luck, rather than planning.

You're not me, though, and you have the benefit of being able to plan your shift to self-employment in advance, so I'm not telling you to hope you get lucky and some money drops out of the sky: I'm telling you to start saving, and to start saving now. (Actually, it would be better if you started saving, like, last year, if I'm honest, but let's just work with what we've got here...) I didn't do that, so it was just fortunate for me that I got my rainy day money some other way: you might get yours in some way other than saving it, too, but all that matters is that you get it. In a way that's legal, obviously.

How much you save is for you to decide, and will depend on your own circumstances, but whatever you do, try to put something away for that proverbial rainy day. Because trust me: it's going to get really, really wet...

THE SECRET TO MAKING
MONEY FROM BLOGGING

So, we're now halfway though part three, and I STILL haven't talked about that blog I started: you know, the one this whole book is supposed to revolve around? What gives?

Well, the fact is that when our business first launched, I had absolutely no idea that blogging was something you could make money from: in fact, it took me years to even realise that the little "online journal" (because that's what we called them back then) I'd started a couple of years earlier could ever be anything more than simply an extension of the paper diaries I'd kept for most of my life.

That "online journal" was called 'Forever Amber', and I'd launched it in 2006, after Terry had his kidney transplant, and we'd decided to finally start planning the wedding that had been put on hold during those dark years of dialysis.

The idea was that I'd use the blog to write about the wedding we were now able to start planning. The business, meanwhile, was, at that point, still a combination of web design (Terry), and copywriting (me). I'd also started to take on some freelance writing work, using the contacts I had from my journalism days to land some regular gigs writing for newspapers, magazines, and, eventually, content-based websites, who would pay me to write what they described as 'SEO articles' - short pieces of content which were written with the specific aim of getting them to rank highly in search engines for certain key words.

Those jobs paid an absolute pittance (as in, the type of rate you'll only accept when you're absolutely desperate - which I was), but I learned a lot about Search Engine Optimisation from them. Without wanting to sound like I'm blowing my own trumpet (I mean, I don't even HAVE my own trumpet), I got pretty good at writing those articles, which the owner of the sites would then have up online within a few hours, earning money.

But how did they earn money, I'm going to pretend I hear you ask? It's a good question, and the short answer is that they earned money by running Google AdSense adverts in the sidebar right next to the articles. Google AdSense is a contextual advertising platform: you basically paste a piece of code into your website, and that code works out what the page is about, and displays an advert to match it. So if I write an article about shoes, say, AdSense will display adverts for shoes, and if I write an article about purple-tailed frogs, AdSense will display adverts for purple-tailed frogs.

AdSense is also a pay-per-click platform, which means the owner of the website the advert appears on gets paid every time someone clicks on the advert. Advertisers "bid" to appear on the top spot on websites, so what you get paid for each click depends on how competitive your subject matter is, and what people are willing to pay to advertise within that niche. In the example above, articles about shoes would probably be matched to fairly high-paying adverts, because there are a lot of people out there searching for shoes. Articles about-purple tailed frogs, on the other hand... well, let's just say they'd be a little less profitable. Because I just made them up.

The websites I was being paid to write for, then, were making their money by publishing articles on subjects a lot of people were interested in (which therefore made those topics profitable), and running AdSense adverts next to them. I'm telling you all of this because, although it might seem very obvious to you if you've been blogging for a long time, it wasn't obvious to me, and if the sheer number of people who ask me how on earth people can make money from blogging is anything to go by, it isn't obvious to a lot of other people, either.

The thing that intrigued me most about the work I was doing back then was that the owners of the websites I was writing for were making money without actually selling anything. There was no physical product to wrap up and send through the post, there were no "customers" to demand that a particular service be delivered on a certain day - there was just a bunch of words on a computer screen, and somehow people like me were getting paid to create them.

Looking back on it now, I'm amazed the penny didn't drop sooner. What I was doing by writing for these content-based websites, you see, was exactly the same thing I'd done as a journalist, working for a free newspaper. Our newspaper didn't sell anything, and people didn't have to pay to read it - it was delivered to their door every week for free, and it made money by selling advertising space on its pages, alongside the stories we wrote.

And that's how you make money from blogging. There's no great secret to it, and the idea isn't a new one - in fact, it's what the publishers of free newspapers and magazines have been doing for decades, only on the internet (which has a much higher profit margin, owing to the fact that websites don't have the pesky printing and distribution overheads a newspaper has). And although a lot of people might resent the comparison, I think it's a really useful way to look at it, because the truth is that starting a blog, with the aim of making money from it, is much the same as starting a newspaper or magazine: in both cases, you work out what people are interested in, or what they want to know, and then you provide them with information on that thing.

Some people are interested in handbags, and some are interested in cars. Some people want to find out how to lower their car insurance quote, and some want to know what shoes they should wear with that dress. Some are probably even interested in purple-tailed frogs, although probably not many. Just me, really, and possibly you, now that I've mentioned them so often.

When enough people are interested in a particular topic, it's possible to make money from that topic - either by selling things that are related to it, or, in this case, writing about the topic and charging people to place adverts alongside what you write. And that's what the owners of the websites I was freelancing for were doing: they were making money by writing content and publishing it on the internet. And if they could do it, then surely I could, too?

After just a few weeks of writing for these sites, you see, I realised I was getting the rough end of the deal. I was doing all the work, and the work I was doing was earning a lot of money - for someone else. That "someone else", however, wasn't doing anything I couldn't do myself - or with Terry's help.

Terry built websites for a living. I wrote content for websites for a living. It's actually pretty embarrassing that it took us so long to work out that if we put those two skills together, we could cut out the middle man, and make money for ourselves - without selling anything, and without having any clients to answer to. And that was exactly what we decided to do.

So the secret to making money from blogging is to work out what people are interested in, and then create content based around those topics. There's a little more to it than that, obviously: you also need to know how, exactly, to monetize the content you're creating,and I'll get to that shortly (or longly, knowing me. Yes, it's a word.), but for now the most important thing to understand about how you'll make money from blogging is that you'll do it by creating a blog that lots of people want to read. Which brings me neatly to our next topic...

HOW I CAME UP WITH A BLOG TOPIC I'M STILL WRITING ABOUT 10 YEARS LATER

Now that I knew it was possible to make money from writing - without having to actually work for someone else, and have them tell me what to write and when - I was totally sold on the idea. To me, it seemed like the closest thing possible to making a living without having a job: and that, after all, was my dream. (Well, that and having a shoe closet like Khloe Kardashian's. Isn't that everyone's dream, though?)

Now, making a living by writing about whatever you want sounds too good to be true, doesn't it? That's because it IS, really. The fact is, it's not enough to just write about whatever it is you happen to be interested in: unless other people are interested in that topic too, no one will want to read what you write, and you won't be able to make any money. Bummer, huh?

As I said back at the start of this book, no one is going to pay you to just go about your life, writing about whatever takes your fancy, and raking in cash and free clothes, purely as a result of being your own, special self. It just doesn't work that way.

No, one of the secrets to successful blogging is to find something to write about that you're passionate about personally, but which other people are interested in too. That could be fashion, it could be beauty, it could be food, parenting, travel - the list goes on. It could even be a combination of more than one of those topics: the most important thing is that it be something you're truly passionate about: because blogging may be the job that doesn't feel like a job, but it still IS one - and if you decide to start a blog on a topic you're not interested in, that will become very obvious, very fast. Congratulations: you've found a way to turn a dream job into a nightmare - you do it by choosing a subject you don't like, and then forcing yourself to write about it every single day! That might make you rich (although it probably won't), but it won't make you happy - and that's what it's all about , right?

I could have started a blog about insurance, or property, or any of the topics I knew were profitable for my clients. I didn't, though, because I knew it would just make me miserable. When you become self-employed, it takes over your life, you see. You have to work harder than you ever did in traditional employment: your entire life ends up revolving around your business, and if your business involves doing something that bores you to tears, well, your whole life will be spent being bored to tears. And who wants that?

What's more, writing about topics you find boring is hard. Not only does it take twice (or three, or four, or five times) as long as writing about a subject you feel passionate about, it becomes impossible to keep on going - and when you blog for a living, you have to be able to keep on going. You have to be able to get up in the morning and come up with a ton of new ideas for things to say about your chosen subject - and then you have to do the same thing the next day, and the day after that, and the day after that, forever. It's hard enough to do that when you are interested in the subject you're writing about, trust me: when it's a subject you're not interested in, it becomes downright impossible.

In my case, I tried blogging about numerous different topics in a bid to find something that would work for me. Over the space of the next few years, I started blogs about:

- Weddings
- Makeup
- Freelance writing
- Shoes
- Ugly items of clothing
- Reality TV

Hell, I even started a blog about my dog at one point. Yes, really. All of these topics were things I was very interested in at the time, but they all had one thing in common: I ran out of steam. And therein lies the problem: most people don't remain interested in the same things forever, and yet many new bloggers assume exactly that, and think that if they start a blog based around whatever their current passion is, they'll be all set. Think about it, though: can you honestly say that you have exactly the same interests now that you did five years ago? How about ten years ago? Fifteen? Do you think you'll have exactly the same interests 20 years from now?

If you were able to answer "yes" to those questions, then I think you've found your niche: congratulations! Now go and start a blog already! Chances are, though, that your interests will change naturally over time, which is why it's a good idea to allow your blog to grow with them, by choosing a topic that isn't too narrow, and a name that will allow you to change direction without totally rebranding.

I decided to name my blog 'Forever Amber', which some people would argue is too vague, because it doesn't tell people exactly what the blog is going to be about. In response to that, however, allow me to submit Amazon.com and Google.com into evidence. I mean, really, they should probably be called

'BigSiteThatSellsEverything.com"
and
"SearchEngineThatWillTakeOverTheWorld.com",   no?

The fact that they're not hasn't exactly held them back, but if you were to name your blog "Mommy of a 2-Year-Old", for instance, you're automatically giving it a one-year shelf-life, because what happens when your toddler is three? What about when he's 12? What happens to that blog you called "The Girl in the Green Shoes" if one day you decide you don't actually LIKE green shoes any more, and would rather wear red ones?

My advice: unless you want your business to be a very short-lived one, or are prepared to rebrand every couple of years, choose a "niche" that's not too restrictive, and a non-specific name. My blog, for instance, has been running for a decade now, and one of the main "secrets" behind its longevity is the fact that I've never tried to force myself to stick to just one "niche". Sure, there are times when I tend to write about one topic more than others, because that's the way life goes - if you're buying a house, say, you're suddenly obsessed with property, and it's all you want to talk about: but once you've moved in, you generally don't continue to browse the property listings and research mortgages online, do you? No, you move on - and my blog has done that too.

Not picking a niche and sticking to it goes against all of the received wisdom of blogging: in fact, I'm willing to bet that most of the other books you've read on blogging have given you the exact opposite of this advice. "Pick a niche!" everyone says, "It's the easiest way to build an audience and make money!" Now, I'm not arguing with that: in fact, I agree that it's easier to build a following when your blog is tightly focused, and people know exactly what to expect. It's much harder to keep that blog going, though, when you have to keep on finding something new to say about that narrow niche you chose, day after day, month after month, year after year. Ultimately, you have to ask yourself if you're running a marathon or a sprint. If it's a sprint, then narrowing your focus will help you get out off the blocks fast, and ahead of your competitors: but if you're running a marathon, then speed can't be your only consideration, can it?

In my case, what I wanted was a business that would last for years: I got it by refusing to settle on just one topic. Instead, I started a "personal" blog, as they were called then (they're now more commonly referred to as 'lifestyle' blogs), which covered a lot of different topics, all of which have one thing in common - they're all things that relate to my life: the things I wear, the products I use, the places I go. You could, I guess, say my niche is myself, but that line was almost too cringeworthy to type, so instead I'll just say that I picked a variety of subjects, all of which have something to connect them.

I might not have a very defined niche, then, but I do believe it's important to have at least some kind of "theme" to connect the subjects you write about. As my blog is a primarily a diary, and I'm writing about my own life, it makes sense for me to also write about what I wear as I go about my life, the products I use, and what I do for a living (blogging, just in case you forgot). Those topics all work together fairly well, because they all tend to appeal to roughly the same audience. What probably wouldn't work so well, on the other hand, would be a blog about tropical fish, say, and quantum physics. Those topics probably won't appeal to the same audience – or if they do, it'll just be pure co-incidence. For the most part, though, the fish lovers will just skip the physics stuff, and the physics buffs won't care so much about the fish, so neither group will be 100% invested in the blog.

So, don't make your niche too narrow: but don't make it too wide, either. Confused? Don't be: the fact is, you'll read endless debates on the the topic of whether blogs need to have a "niche", but there's really no right or wrong answer to that. What works for one person might not work for another, so my best advice is to not worry too much about narrowing your niche, and to concentrate instead on identifying your passions in life, and then finding a way to connect them.

I picked my blog topics through a long process of trial and error. You're not me, though, so you get to sit down and think about:

- What kind of things you're interested in.

- What kind of things you're good at.

- What kind of things you have a degree of knowledge about that other people might not have.

Write down your answers to these questions: if the list is a short one, you have your "niche". If it's a long one, you have the categories your more general blog will cover. If you don't even HAVE a list, meanwhile? Well, I've two suggestions for you:

1. Don't start a blog.

I know, probably not what you were expecting to hear in a book designed to help you make a living from blogging, huh? The thing is, though, I'm a businesswoman, not an evangelist. I LOVE blogging, and I couldn't imagine doing anything else:

I'm not stupid, though (please resist the urge to comment on that statement): I know blogging isn't for everyone, and I also know that the best blogs out there are the ones written by people who really have a passion for their subject. The ones who wake up every morning with something to say, and who can't even be bothered waiting until after breakfast to say it. Those people generally don't have trouble deciding what to blog about, and they don't struggle for blog post ideas, either: far from it.

That's not, of course, to say that someone who doesn't have the burning desire to write about a particular topic can't possibly run a profitable blog: I mean, I'm sure the owner of a successful cleaning business doesn't wake up every morning thinking, "Wow, I just can't wait to get out there and clean other people's houses! I'm not even going to stop to grab a cup of coffee first!" Nevertheless, she's a businesswoman: she came up with an idea she thought would work, researched it, and now she has a thriving business - not because cleaning was a hobby that she decided to make a living from, but because that's the way life works, isn't it? We don't all have a "passion" for the things we do for a living, but it doesn't necessarily stop us making a success of them.

Having said all of that, though, I'm going to put my Debbie Downer hat on here and suggest that bloggers, unlike cleaners, or many other professions, DO tend to find most success when they really enjoy what they do. You don't have to love cleaning to be able to do a great job of it, and you don't have to love writing to be able to string a grammatically correct sentence together. With blogging, however, if you don't love it, it normally shows: and one of the ways it shows is in a lack of inspiration. If you've racked your brain for days, and you REALLY can't think of anything you want to write about, then, I'm going to gently suggest that blogging might not be the right career choice for you. (No, you're not getting a refund on the book...)

I have one other suggestion, however:

2. Start a lifestyle blog

The phrase 'lifestyle blog' is one that's loosely applied to just about every blog these days. Mostly, it's used to describe blogs which focus primarily on the author's life: what they eat, where they go, how they decorate their homes, what they wear - the list goes on. If you feel that you have a passion for writing, but you can't narrow it down to just one topic (or even a handful of topics), consider filing your blog under the 'lifestyle' banner - for now, at least.

By giving yourself license to write about whatever you like, you'll give yourself the chance to work out what you actually DO like. That might not necessarily be the topic you expected to want to write about (Which is why I strongly advise keeping the name of your blog suitably vague), but sometimes the best way to work out what you want to write about is by ... writing. About everything. Sooner or later you'll start to notice similar themes or ideas coming up more and more often: there will be some posts you feel really enthused about, and others you put off writing, because you just can't motivate yourself, and you might not know what those topics are until you try.

When I started my beauty blog, for instance, I thought I was going to LOVE writing about makeup, but, as I quickly discovered, that just wasn't the case: sure, I loved USING makeup... just not enough to fill an entire blog with posts about it. I really struggled to motivate myself to write that blog, and eventually closed it down altogether, because I realised it was never going to work. I do still write about makeup occasionally: but I do it on my "lifestyle" blog, which means I only have to write about makeup when there's something I WANT to write about it. The rest of the time, I write about other things: that works for me, but it might not work for you. As I said, you sometimes won't know until you try...

THE SECRETS OF SUCCESSFUL BLOG DESIGN

One of the things that holds a lot of new bloggers back is the idea that blogging should be free. You can, after all, set up a blog in about five minutes or so, using a free platform like Blogspot or Wordpress.com. Those platforms come with a range of templates which you can instantly apply to your blog, without any design or technical knowledge whatsoever: why, then, would you choose to hire a web designer, or pay to self-host your website, when there's absolutely no need to?

Yeah, that's what I thought, too.

I started my first blog on a free platform (or close to free, anyway: I used Typepad, which charged a few pounds per month, but which was easy to use, and looked pretty swish - or so I thought.), using one of the stock templates they provided. And then, a year or so later, I had to go through all of the hassle and headaches of moving the site to a self-hosted Wordpress installation.

Why?

Because free blogging platforms are easy to use, and they do the job, but they're not the ideal place to launch a profit-making business: it's as simple as that. And yes, I know - you have a list of famous bloggers who use Blogspot or Tumblr, and it hasn't done THEM any harm, has it? Well, maybe not: but I can guarantee it won't have done them much good, either, and I can also guarantee that they're the exceptions, rather than the rule.

The fact is that most of the big-name bloggers DON'T use free services or stock themes. Why would they? If they're serious about turning their blog into a business, they probably don't want to limit its potential or make it look exactly the same as all of the other blogs out there, and that's what free services do. Sure, you can customise a Blogspot template, or pay someone to create a custom theme for you, but ultimately you'll be limited in what you can actually do with that blog: in the case of Wordpress.com, for instance (not to be confused with Wordpress.org, which is the self-hosted version of the platform), you're even limited in terms of the type of advertising your blog can carry - not a great idea for a business, huh?

I'm not saying this to knock platforms like Wordpress.com or Blogspot, by the way: they're excellent services, and can be a great way to learn how to blog, without having to invest any money in it. If I could do it all again, however, I'd skip that "messing around with a free platform" stage, and proceed straight to self-hosting. I use Wordpress for all of my blogs, and I use it because there are literally no limitations as to what I can do with it. If I decide I want to add a specific feature, chances are there'll be a plugin I can download and use - and, if there isn't, there'll be someone who can code it for me.

What's more, by choosing to self-host, I fully own my blog, and my business. If I were to use Blogspot, say, I'm kind of at their mercy. If they suddenly decide to close down (Unlikely, I know, but stranger things have happened...), I could lose everything. Similarly, if Blogspot decided my blog had broken one of their rules, they could simply remove it from their platform - and take my livelihood with it.

Ultimately, then, it's basically the decision whether to rent or buy. There are advantages to both, obviously, but for me - and for the majority of other full-time bloggers - the advantages of owning your own home - er, I mean blog - and being able to totally control your business, far outweigh the downsides of having to mow the lawn, clear the gutters, and be responsible for all of that pesky maintenance.

As for the design of the site, well, design isn't my strong point, which is why I married a web designer. What? Why are you looking at me like that? You don't think that's romantic? OK, OK, I'm kidding - I didn't marry Terry for his web design skills, but I have to admit, they DO come in handy. In my case, once the free templates, with headers hastily thrown together using Paintshop Pro, had lost their appeal, I decided it was time to pony-up for a much more professional looking theme, which I then begged Terry to customise for me. And then to re-customise. And maybe a third, fourth and fifth time, just for luck. (He tells me I'm his most difficult customer: I believe it...)

"That's good for you, Amber," I hear you say, "But what about those of us who don't have a handy web designer on call 24/7?" Worry not: you can, of course, hire one fairly easily, but if you feel like having a go at designing your own blog, there are tons of pre-made themes available, which will allow you to create a professional looking blog, without much in the way of design knowledge. Of course, as time goes on, you might want to customise the look of your blog even further, but purchasing a ready-made theme is where most bloggers start out, and there's nothing wrong with that.

To help you decide what you want your blog to look like, here's (more or less) everything I've learned about blog design:

GOOD DESIGN IS LARGELY SUBJECTIVE

One of the first things I learned about blog design is that you can't please everyone. In fact, in my case, I can't even please myself: my blog has had dozens of different looks over the decade it's been online, and no sooner do I settle on one I like, I start wanting to change it. Here's a little secret for you, though: I've had complaints about every single one of my blog designs.

Literally every single one. Almost as soon as a new design goes live, I'll start getting comments from people saying they preferred the last one - and handily forgetting that they hated that one when IT went live, too. It can be quite disheartening to spend time working on your design, and getting it exactly the way you like it, only for people to instantly start nit-picking over colours, and fonts, and almost everything else you can think of, but the main thing you'll learn from this is that "good" design is subjective. No matter WHAT you do, someone out there will HATE it - and want to tell you all about it. As Dita Von Teese once said, "You could be the ripest, juciest peach in the world, and there's still going to be someone who hates peaches."

So it is with blog design: and the sooner you realise that, the sooner you can stop stressing over every little detail, and move onto the next point, which is the most important one:

USABILITY ISN'T SUBJECTIVE

Ultimately, what your blog looks like is less important than how it works. Many bloggers - myself included - forget this, and spent hours fretting over making it look just right, when the fact is that all your readers really care about is whether or not they can read the thing. Well, that IS the whole point, after all, isn't it?

Here's how to make sure people can read your blog:

1. Keep it clean

People have lots and lots of different preferences for how they like blogs to look. One thing most people seem to agree on, however, is that they like the layout to be clean, uncluttered, and easy to navigate. And I know: it's really, really tempting to cram your template and sidebar with every widget known to the internet. Twitter! Instagram! Facebook! Blog buttons! Animated gifts! Pictures of cats! The kitchen sink!

While it's nice to have a great-looking blog, however, readers come for the content, not for the awesome font you used in the header, or the images in your sidebar. There's nothing wrong with a site with "character", but it's better to try and do that without adding too much clutter.

Right now, the fashion (and yes, there are fashions in blog design, just like in anything else) is for very minimal designs, with lots of white space. You don't have to make your blog look like that if you don't want to (and there's a good argument for taking it in a different direction, and making it stand out), but regardless of the look and feel you end up going for, it's a good idea to cut the clutter, and only include those elements you think will actually be useful to your readers.

2. Keep it clear

I've said it already, but I'll say it again: when you're designing your site, the most important thing of all is that you make it easy for people to read and navigate it – and that means ALL people, including those who are visually impaired. Text and background colours are of the utmost importance here, and regardless of your personal taste, dark-coloured text on a light-coloured background is by far the easiest to read.

Light-coloured text on a dark background, on the other hand, can be almost impossible: if I come across a blog which uses white text on black, for instance, I'll instantly hit the "back" button, because that can actually trigger a migraine for me – something about those scrolling white lines completely messes with my brain.

Font size and style is also important here, and while the existence of Google Fonts makes it tempting to use some fancy, flowing script for your post text, that's only a good idea if you don't want people to actually read what you write. Those fonts look pretty in headers and as titles, but for your actual posts, it's better to stick to something clear and easy to read: fonts like Ariel, Helvetica and Times New Roman might seem "boring", but are popular for a reason.

Similarly, make sure your text is large enough to be readable, and dark enough to be seen. For some reason, I keep coming across blogs (particularly fashion blogs) with teeny-tiny writing, in a pale shade of grey. It makes my eyes hurt, so can you imagine how someone with a visual impairment would feel trying to read it?

3. Keep it consistent

This is possibly one of those "goes-without-saying" things, but keeping your design consistent across all of the pages of your site will give it a more cohesive, professional feel. Choose the colours you want to use for your text, logo, headings, etc, and then use them consistently. I also recommend making sure all of your photos are the same width as each other, and as the text below/above them. You'll rarely find a successful blog – particularly a fashion or beauty blog – which uses tiny images, so don't be afraid to make your images big enough to be seen. On that note, though…

4. Keep it quick

How quickly your blog loads is just as important as how it looks. The problem is that many of the design elements which help make a site visually distinctive, can also really slow it down. Huge images, lots of widgets, tons of pointless clutter – all of those things will make your blog slow to load, and it doesn't matter HOW good it looks if people don't hang around to wait to see it (and trust me, they won't....).

5. Keep it compatible

This tip is perhaps one of the most important, and it's about making sure your blog is compatible with different browsers and mobile devices. A lot of people make the mistake of testing their design only on the browser/monitor or device they use personally, forgetting that different people use different browsers, differently sized monitors, different resolutions, etc. An increasing number of visitors will also be viewing your blog on their phone or tablet (I do almost all of my blog reading on my phone, these days...), so it's really important to make sure they can actually SEE it.

This all sounds complicated, and can BE complicated if you're the one coding the site from scratch. Luckily, most of us don't have to do that: most bloggers simply buy a ready-made theme and many of those themes are designed to be compatible with different browsers, and fully responsive, so they can be viewed on different screens or devices.

When you're looking for a theme, always, always go for a responsive one. Responsive themes change size so that no matter the size of the screen you're viewing the blog on, it will still display properly. For instance, if you look at my blog (ForeverAmber.co.uk, just in case you forgot...) on a wide-screen monitor, you'll see the post plus sidebar (or three rows of posts, if you're looking at the homepage). If you view it on an iPhone, however, you'll see a variation of the design, which still looks much the same, but which fits into the much smaller screen available for it. With a non-responsive design, all you see on an iPhone is whichever part of the site fits on the screen - normally a part of the header and a small section of the post: not good for readers.

6. Give it some character

So you have your clean, clear, compatible template – the only thing remaining is to give it some character, to make it stand out from all of the OTHER clean white blogs out there. There are lots of ways to add identity to a blog theme, but I'd say the most important one is to get yourself a decent logo/banner, and make consistent use of colours and fonts throughout the site. You might also want to consider using these same "branding" elements on your social media, too, to make your brand even more memorable.

4

HOW I CREATE FRESH CONTENT ALMOST EVERY DAY

THE MISTAKE MOST NEW BLOGGERS MAKE

I have some bad news for you. You know everything you just learned in the last chapter? All that stuff about choosing a blog name and topic, setting up your website and getting it looking exactly the way you want it?

All of that's the easy bit.

The mistake a lot of new bloggers make is in thinking that's the hard part. They view starting a blog almost like climbing a mountain, and once they've got that blog up and running, they think they've reached the summit: then they stand there wondering why the readers aren't flocking to them, why brands aren't clamoring to advertise on that shiny new blog they just spent weeks perfecting - as if all they have to do is turn up, and be rewarded for it. Well, here's the harsh truth: it doesn't work that way. No one is going to pay you just to turn up: or to do the same things, in the same way, as everyone else.

What people are going to pay you for is to be exceptional: to not just launch a blog and update it occasionally with pictures of your cat, but to take really, really good pictures of your cat, and to then write about your cat in a way that will make people really care about him. To want to see YOUR cat more than anyone else's cat. To be intensely interested in everything your cat does - so much so that they'll want to tell other people about your cat too, to the point where brands will start to take notice and say, "You know what, we really need to be a part of this whole 'cat' thing."

THAT'S what you have to do in order to make a living from blogging, and that's not nearly as easy as simply installing Wordpress and choosing a theme was. I mean, I WISH.

So, how do you create content that people will love?

Well, first of all, you have to find out what people love. Again, it sounds obvious, but again, it really isn't, because rather than finding out what people might want to read on their blog, a lot of new bloggers just assume they know the answer, and then they write that. I mean, people will want to see pictures of your cat, right? It's obvious, really: your cat is super-cute, he's really friendly, and he does this funny thing with his paw that ... you'd really have to see it. As I said above, however, people aren't going to care about your cat just because you tell them to, and they're not going to care just because YOU do. So, let's talk some more about cats, shall we?

HOW TO MAKE PEOPLE CARE ABOUT YOUR CAT

When I say I want to talk about cats, I don't mean that literally, obviously. I mean, cats are awesome and all, but you're really here to find out how to make a living from blogging, aren't you? The thing is, though, making a blog successful really is like trying to interest thousands of people in photos of your cat: and now I AM talking literally - to some of you, at least.

Even bloggers who aren't just posting photos of their cats (or their meals, or their outfits, or whatever it is they've decided to make the main topic of their blog), are essentially doing the same thing: they're trying to take their chosen subject matter and make people want to read about it - and to read about it from THEM, rather than from someone else. So, how do you do that?

In other words: how do you make people care about your cat?

To answer this question, I'm going to stick with the cat analogy a little longer, and assume you all understand that I'm not REALLY talking about cats. (Er, you do understand that I'm not actually talking about cats, right?)

Here's how to make people care about your cat...

1. Have a cat.

Well, hello, Capt'n obvious here, reporting for duty! It sounds super-obvious, but if you want to make people care about your cat, you have to actually have a damn cat in the first place. In blogging terms, this means that you have to have something to say. As strange at it might sound, quite a lot of people don't stop to think about what they have to say. They don't look at their lives, their interests, their knowledge-base, and ask themselves what they have that might make them interesting to someone else - instead, they just look at what everyone else is doing, and try to do that, instead. "No one's reading my blog!" they cry. "I'm trying so hard, and I'm still not getting any visitors! WAH!"

Normally when I see bloggers saying things like that, I'll go and take a look at their blog, and find the same things I can find anywhere else: they'll maybe have done a 'What's in My Handbag' post, say, or a 'What I Got Up To This Weekend' one. Now, there's absolutely nothing wrong with either of those topics, obviously: I've written similar ones myself, and I've happily read them on other blogs.

What these new bloggers are failing to realise, however, is that it's not enough to show people what's in your handbag: you have to first of all give them a reason to CARE about what you might be carrying around all day. Ultimately, people will only be interested in the contents of your handbag if they're interested in YOU: so before you can start writing blog posts about what you've done and what you've bought, you're going to have to lay a bit of groundwork by showing them who you are, and giving them a reason to care about your life/opinions/thoughts.

If you DON'T do that, it's the blogging equivalent of walking up to a stranger at a party, thrusting a photo of your cat in their face, and expecting them to want to hear aaaaalll about him. So many bloggers do this: they just jump right in without stopping to consider what they can bring to the blogging party, that will make all of the other party-goers stop what they're doing and come over to take a look. In other words, they don't have a cat.

2. Have a cat that's different from all the other cats.

So, you have a cat: good for you. Your next problem, then, is that you're not the only one: lots of people have cats. Cats are everywhere - and so are blogs, these days. Back when I started blogging, it was such a niche thing that hardly anyone even knew what a blog WAS. Nowadays bloggers are on the news, in the papers - hell, they're even on the last LiveAid single. (And, OK, technically those are vloggers, but they're all just different breeds of cat, aren't they?) So, how do you make sure your cat - er, your blog - is different from everyone else's?

Look, I'm not saying you need to re-invent the wheel here. You don't have to create an entirely new concept, or even to do something no one else has ever done before - although if you CAN do that, then more power to you: don't forget to call when you make your first million!

Instead, you just need to find your OWN way to do things. Lots of people don't bother to do this either: instead, they simply start blogs, and then put a lot of effort into making them virtually indistinguishable from every other site on Bloglovin'. Same layout. Same colours. Same regular posts. (How many "Friday Favourites" have you see this week, be honest?) They could almost all be the same person, couldn't they?

People do this, of course, because they believe it's the way to be successful. If it works for other people, it'll surely work for you too, right?

Well, not necessarily. If you look at the most successful bloggers out there, you'll tend to find that they're the ones who set trends rather than following them: the ones who have something about them that helps set them apart from the crowd. It could be their writing style. It could be their personal style. It could even be the colour of their hair, or the fact that they always wear hats. It could be anything, really, and the important thing to note here is that, again, you don't have to be the only blogger in the whole world who has that colour of hair, or a particular turn of phrase: you just have to find a way to make your blog identifiable as YOURS, rather than blending in with everyone else's.

Why should I read your post instead of someone else's? If you can't answer this question, you probably need to re-think why you're even bothering to post it, and if your time might be better spent coming up with an idea that's really different, and really YOU. People don't normally become successful simply by following the crowd, and making sure they're exactly the same as everyone in it, so find your own perspective, your own style, your own way of doing things, and your blog will be better for it.

3. Have a cat with a personality.

One of the things that makes blogs different from the rest of the media is that blogs usually have some kind of personality behind them, so you get to know the person behind all of those words and pictures. When you speak to blog readers, you'll often find that this is the thing that keeps them coming back to particular blogs they like: they might have originally started following the blog because they liked the person's personal style, enjoyed their recipes, or found their advice useful, but they continue following the blog because they feel like they get to know the person behind the clothes, food and advice posts. They want to know more about that person: to follow their story, to get an insight into their lives - even to look at photos of their cats, if that's what the blogger is offering.

Despite this, a lot of new bloggers work very hard to remove every scrap of personality from their blogs. They do this, partly using the method described above, where they seek to make their blog as homogeneous as possible, but they also do it by refusing to just be themselves: by writing in a way that sounds more like a magazine article or even a high school book report, than allowing some personality to shine through, or by adopting a very impersonal tone when writing posts or interacting with their readers. Some people even hide their faces, or cut their heads out of outfit photos - and who can really relate to some strange, headless wonder?

Now, privacy is important: I'm not saying it isn't, and some people have very good reasons why they might not want their readers to know about their lives - or even to know their real name, or what they look like. If you're one of those people, it's important to know first of all that you are absolutely entitled to your privacy: it's a good idea to protect it, and you should never feel pressured into revealing something online that makes you feel uncomfortable. Ever.

The second thing you have to understand, however, is that if you're not giving away ANYTHING of your personality, you'll make it very hard for people to relate to you, or to care much about you. Why would I care about your cat, after all, if I've never seen it, and I don't even know its name? I won't, is the short answer to that: and I also won't care much about a blogger who's a completely closed book. I might still visit their site occasionally, to try out their recipes or see their shopping recommendations, but I won't be truly invested in it: I won't recommend it to other people, I won't visit every day, and I probably won't comment on or share their posts, either. I'll be a half-hearted reader at best, and no one wants that, do they? Doesn't your cat deserve better?

If you think he does, then do your best to show me WHY. Don't just tell me you have a cat and expect me to care about it: give me reasons to care about your cat by showing me his personality, and letting me get to know him. And by "him", I obviously mean YOU.

(Unless your blog really IS about your cat, obviously.)

4. Have a helpful cat.

There are all kinds of cats in the world, and there are different types of blog post, too, all of which have different purposes. Some are designed purely to entertain people, some are there to document an experience, others are just things the author found interesting and hoped others would, too. Each of these different post types are valuable in their own way, and it's a good idea to have a mixture of them on your blog. When it comes to actually growing your blog, and gaining more traffic, however, the posts that are most likely to do that are the ones which attempt to help people. That could be a tutorial or 'how to' piece, it could be a list of tips or advice, or it could simply be inspiration, in the form of an outfit or recipe which people can try for themselves: the important thing is to ask yourself what the reader will get out of your post and if it will help them in some way.

If you're struggling to think of a way to write helpful content, go back to those questions in the previous chapter: ask yourself what you're good at, and what you're interested in, and try to figure out how to use that knowledge and passion to answer someone's question, or show them how to do something. You don't have to write these kinds of posts exclusively, but they're the kind of posts that get shared, so writing them when you can will really help your blog.

5. Keep improving your cat.

Back in the days when I first launched my blog, things were very different. Most blogs didn't have a lot of photos on them, for instance, and the ones you did find tended to be small, grainy, and taken from a million miles away. Templates were very basic: you'd find hundreds of blogs which all looked exactly the same, and no one really cared what their blog looked like anyway, because content is king, right?

Well, content IS king - I'm not going to argue with that. But we now live in an age where appearance matters more than ever - and blogging isn't exempt from that, no matter how much you might wish it was. As you start to dip your toe into the blogging waters, you'll come across a lot of bloggers talking about how they miss the "good old days", when blogs were still a little rough around the edges, people took mirror selfies on their phones, and everything had a very "homemade" feel to it, as opposed to the magazine-style look that many blogs have these days.

If you're one of the people who likes to talk about those "good old days", I have some bad news for you: they're not coming back. The internet is a different place today than it was five years ago, and it'll be different again a year from now. This isn't a popular opinion, but the bloggers who succeed tend to be the ones who move with the times: who keep striving to learn new skills, to make improvements to their sites and their content, and to adapt to the changing face of the internet. The reason for this is simple: that's what works.

The fact is, people might say they long for the days of blurry images and bad graphics, but if that was what they really wanted, those would be the bloggers who were currently enjoying the most success. They're not, though: if you look at some of the most successful blogs in the world, you'll see that one thing they all have in common is the fact that they all look amazing, with clear, brightly-lit photos, and an easy-to-navigate template.

They say you shouldn't judge a book by a cover, or a blog by its appearance - but the fact is, people DO. It's one of those things that people don't want to hear, but if you really want to blog for a living, work on your photography, invest in a professional looking design, and never stop learning and improving. Or, you know, you could just stick to that free theme that's exactly the same as hundreds of other blogs, and take blurry mirror shots of your outfits, in conditions so dark that no one can actually see what you're wearing: up to you.

6. Pay close attention to what your cat is up to.

It's also fashionable right now for bloggers to say that it's "not all about the numbers" and that you shouldn't pay too much attention to your stats. Actually, though, if your blog is your livelihood, and you're depending on it to pay your mortgage every month, then sorry to break it to you, but it IS all about the numbers, and if you're not paying attention to your cat - I mean your stats - you're not giving yourself the opportunity to figure out what's working for you, and what isn't so successful.

You HAVE to look at your stats. I'm not saying you have to actively obsess over them - bear in mind that you'll have good months and bad months, and there won't always be a whole lot you can do about them - but you do have to keep a close eye on how well your blog is doing, and use the information in your analytics to make changes when they're required.

7. Make your cat consistent.

My final point is also one of the most important: I have no statistics to back this up, unfortunately, but I have a strong hunch that one of the main reasons most blogs fail is because their authors give up on them before they've really had a chance. Another reason is that they're just not consistent: they go for weeks without updating their blog, then publish five new articles in a week, before going back to radio silence - and then they wonder why they're not successful.

When you look at the blogs that ARE successful, however,

you'll normally see two things:

1. Consistency

2. Longevity

Successful bloggers don't just blog occasionally, or give up at the first hurdle. They keep on going, putting out quality content on a regular basis, and continuing to do it for years on end. You don't just feed your cat when you feel like it, after all, and if your cat is sick, you wouldn't just give up on it. (At least, I hope not.) Now, I'm not saying your blog is like a cat, here, but ... actually, you know what? Your blog is like a cat. Sometimes it'll be the kind of cat that hisses when you get close to it, and expects you to keep on looking after it, even although it won't even let you stroke it, but you can't give up on it, and you can't give up on your blog either - or think you can neglect it, and still expect it to perform.

You can't be a successful blogger, in other words, if you don't have a well-cared for blog. And I'm going to stop talking about cats now, I promise.

AMBER McNAUGHT

5

WHERE I GET IDEAS
FOR BLOG POSTS

THE TWO TYPES OF CONTENT
SUCCESSFUL BLOGGERS WRITE

There are dozens of different styles of blog post you could choose to write: dozens. Maybe even hundreds, actually - not that I've tried to count them. Luckily, though, all of these hundreds of different styles of post can be roughly divided into two different types:

A) EVERGREEN CONTENT
and
B) EVERYTHING ELSE

(Yes, that IS the technical term...)

Evergreen content is ... well, it's exactly what it sounds like, basically: content that remains ever "green" – by which I mean ever relevant, ever helpful, ever in date. Evergreen content forms the basis of your entire blog: these posts are normally timeless, so they don't go out of date the way a news article would, say, and they're the kind of posts that people will still be reading and finding relevant days, weeks, and hopefully even years from now.

This type of content is distinct from all of the other posts you might publish, because all of that other stuff WILL tend to date sooner or later. News is a prime example of this: no one's interested in reading yesterday's news, and they're even less interested in reading last year's news, so if you're writing a post with an "expiry date", so to speak, it will probably only be of interest to people on the day or week it's published, before quietly sinking into your blog's archive, where it'll be forgotten unless someone happens to stumble upon it one day.

Lots of the posts bloggers write will fall into this second category: a post about what you got up to over the weekend, for instance, probably won't still be getting traffic years from now, and even outfit posts will date after a while - because what you wore three years ago isn't particularly relevant to today's readers, is it? That doesn't, however, mean you shouldn't ever write those posts: sites which don't contain much/ any evergreen content CAN work (news and gossip sites are a good example of this type of website), but because their content tends to date quickly, and to only be of interest in the days and weeks after it's published, those sites require a constant stream of new content to replace them, and keep their audience coming back.

So it is with your blog. If you only ever publish short, time-sensitive updates, you might attract readers, but you'll have to work really hard at keeping them, by constantly coming up with new posts to replace the ones that are no longer relevant. If, on the other hand, you add in some useful, non time-sensitive content to go along with those "newsy" pieces, those posts will have a much better chance of becoming "evergreen", and they'll continue to attract visitors to your blog, even on days when you don't have something new to post.

The types of posts that become evergreen tend to be the ones that people will find useful in some way: so, tutorials and 'How to' type articles work well, as do reviews or other informational pieces that people might be looking for information on. For instance, here are the titles of the five most viewed posts on my blog:

1. How to do a messy bun (Over 5 years old)

2. How to walk in high heels (Over 1 year old)

3. The best foundations for pale skin (Over 6 years old)

4. Sleep-in Rollers Review (Over 2 years old)

5. My Makeup Storage (Over 1 year old)

Notice anything? These articles are the most viewed posts on my blog every month without fail, and as you can see, they all have one thing in common: they provide information, or help people solve a problem. Because of that, they're "evergreen" - and they'll hopefully STILL be bringing visitors to my blog years from now.

You don't have to ONLY write evergreen content, either, though: while some bloggers prefer to spend their time exclusively writing these longer, more timeless pieces, others like to mix them up with the "newsy" style posts which might not be popular forever, but which can be fun to read, equally fun to write, and which are often a good way to keep readers interested and engaged, while you work on those longer pieces of content.

Which post style you favour will, of course, be up to you, and the type of posts you write will also depend on what your aim is with each post. Do you want the post to get lots of comments? To rank highly in search engines? To be shared on social media? Whatever your aim, it will play a large part in helping you determine what type of blog post(s) you write: here's a quick look at some different types of post, and how they'll work for your blog...

HOW TO WRITE POSTS THAT DO WELL IN SEARCH ENGINES

One of the first types of post you're likely to be interested in are the posts that rank highly in search engines like Google, and which bring visitors to your site.

So, how do you work out which posts will do well in search engines?

If you're thinking the answer to this is going to something horribly complicated, probably involving the phrase "search engine optimisation", relax: we're not quite there. Yet. We WILL get there soon, but for now, all you need to know is that there's a difference between making sure your blog posts show up in search engines - "search engine optimisation" - and knowing what kind of blog posts people use search engines to find.

The first of those options does, indeed, require you to have some knowledge of how search engines work. The second, however, only requires you to have used a search engine yourself at some point: simple, huh?

If you think about the kind of thing you use search engines to find, you'll probably realise you mostly use Google et al to find answers or information. So, you might search for the best restaurant in your area, say, or information on how to style your hair a particular way. Other times, you might be looking for something to buy, or just something to entertain you: my point is that when you go to a search engine, you're looking for something SPECIFIC. And that "something specific" tends NOT to be "stories about what random bloggers got up to this weekend".

As a blogger, then, this DOESN'T mean that you shouldn't ever write rambling stories about your life: those stories could be useful for your blog in other ways, and we'll get to that soon - along with the SEO, and all of the other stuff I keep promising you. (Don't worry, I'm keeping a list...) What it does mean, however, is that if you ONLY write those kind of blog posts, you probably won't get many visitors from search engines: because that's just not what people tend to be searching for.

How do you know what they ARE searching for? There are a couple of ways to do this. One is to look at Google's Keyword Planner: this was actually designed to help Google advertisers work out which keywords they should "bid" on when they're creating adverts, and it does this by telling them what people are searching for. If that information is useful to advertisers, it's obviously useful to you as a blogger, too, and you can basically log-in, type a word related to your blog topic ("fashion", say, or "dresses"), and get a list of keywords related to that term, which you can then use to come up with a blog post idea. So if you notice that people are searching for "cheap red dresses", say, you might write a post called 'Where to find cheap red dresses", "My favourite red dress" or "ten of the best red dresses" - you get the idea.

There are other websites which are designed to perform similar functions (just Google the phrase "keyword tool" to find them), and there's also a pretty good Wordpress plugin called 'YOAST SEO', which does a similar thing. While these keyword tools can be useful, however, another easy way to come up with topics which are likely to bring you visitors from search engines is to simply ask yourself what kind of questions someone might have about your chosen topic, or how you can help them. Again, this comes back to the basics of choosing a topic:

- **What are you good at?**
- **What do you know a lot about?**
- **What do people ask you about?**

The answers to these questions will give you a bunch of ideas for topics people might use a search engine to find information on. The key here is to create content that's USEFUL to people in some way. That could mean:

A tutorial on how to do something (cook a certain dish, paint your house, create a hairstyle). If there's something you can do well enough to be able to help other people with it, chances are that someone out there will want to know how to do it too.

A review of a product, place, service, etc. People are always looking for honest opinions about products they're thinking of buying, places they're considering visiting, restaurants they might want to try, and so on. Think of all of the things you've done lately: there must be some kind of review potential in there somewhere, no?

Anything else that helps someone, or provides then with information. This is vastly over-simplifying things, of course, but the easiest way to work out what this might mean for your blog is to ask yourself what YOU might use a search engine to find out about your blog niche. If you can't think of anything, because you obviously (obviously!) picked a topic you ALREADY know a lot about, then go back to the beginning and ask yourself what you might have searched for when you were just starting to get interested in your chosen topic: those basic questions might sound obvious to you, but they won't be obvious to everyone - and they could provide the perfect jumping-off topic for your blog posts.

In other words, the type of content that does well in search engines is normally EVERGREEN content: so it's worth spending some time on creating posts that fit that description.

HOW TO WRITE POSTS THAT GET LOTS OF COMMENTS

One of the best things about blogging is that it allows you to get instant feedback on your posts, and interaction from your readers, thanks to the handy little "comments" box that appears at the end of your posts.
Comments are hugely important to bloggers: they're how we know people are reading our work, and, more importantly, what they thought of it. Stats, after all, only tell you so much: your blog analytics will tell you how many people visited your blog that day, and which posts they looked at, but they won't tell you if they liked what they saw, or whether they even read it. Comments from readers do all of that, and a little more besides, which is why bloggers set so much store by them.

Unfortunately, however, comments are much less important to

readers than they are to bloggers. Thanks to the advent of social media, many bloggers are finding it harder and harder to encourage people to leave comments on their posts: why would they, after all, when it's so much easier to simply "like" it on Facebook, or "heart" it on Twitter? Bloggers these days have to work much harder than they used to in order to get feedback from their readers, and one of the things you can do is to think carefully about the type of posts you're writing. Here are some posts that are more likely to generate comments for you:

Opinion pieces.

Standard advice would be that the more controversial your opinion, the more comments you'll get, but I'd advise against controversy-for-controversy's sake – it comes off as trolling, and tends to create drama, so if you're going to be controversial, then a) only write it if you genuinely believe it, and b) understand that you'll get a response, but you might not like it!

Personal anecdotes, especially the type of posts people find honest or relatable.

I find that readers respond well to posts which strike a chord with them – it can be scary to share something personal to you, but sometimes the posts where you're admitting a weakness, or talking about something you've struggled with will be the ones that are best received. In my case, I've written posts about being an introvert, and about the hateful - and occasionally hilarious - comments people have made about my red hair: those are some of the most-commented posts I've ever written, as well as being some of the most satisfying - it's always reassuring to write about something that's happened to you, and have people respond to say, "Me too!"

List posts.

I've written about the 12 things redheads are sick of hearing, 5 things to do in Scotland, and 9 things you should never say to someone: these are similar to the opinion pieces I mentioned above, and, like those, they tend to generate a lot of discussion.

Requests for advice.

Sometimes if you want people to comment, you have to ASK them to: not by saying "Hey, everyone, please comment on this post!" - I mean, that could sound just a little bit desperate - but by asking questions, or requesting advice. Most people love to give advice, so even posts which don't specifically ASK for it, but which people CAN offer advice on, will tend to get comments: i.e. when I write about what I've been watching on Netflix, people will often want to offer their own suggestions.

WHY I WRITE LONG POSTS, EVEN ALTHOUGH PEOPLE TELL ME NOT TO

One final word on creating content, before we move on: exactly how long should your blog posts be, anyway?

You're probably going to hate me for this, but I'm afraid it's another vague answer:

Your posts should be exactly as long as they need to be, and no longer.

Helpful, huh?

I'm being totally serious, though: when you start blogging, you'll read a lot of advice on the subject of the ideal length for a blog post, and this advice tends to fall into one of two camps:

1. People who think you should keep your posts as concise as possible, because blog readers have short attention spans, and aren't willing to wade through lengthy pieces of text, especially on a computer screen.

2. People who say long content ranks better in search engines, because it tends to contain more information (plus more keywords), and therefore be more useful.

Let's make this is as simple as possible, then: both of these groups are wrong.

Well, let me re-phrase that: they're not TOTALLY wrong. It's correct to say that some readers dislike long blog posts, and just won't read them: but that doesn't mean that ALL readers are like that, or that NONE of them will read a longer post. Actually, the very longest posts on my blog are also the ones which have attracted the most comments, so any time someone tries to tell me no one will read my longer posts, I simply thank them for their advice, and keep right on doing what I'm doing: because I know it works.

It's also true to say that longer posts tend to rank higher in search engines, for exactly the reasons given. Search engines essentially rank websites in order of their usefulness to readers, and the longer a post is, the more useful it's likely to be. That doesn't, however, mean that ALL posts need to be long ones, or that a longer post will always be better than a short one, however. In fact, some forms of content work better when you keep them short and to the point: someone visiting my shoe blog, for instance, probably doesn't want to read 5,000 words about a pair of shoes, do they? No, they just want to see the shoes, find out enough about them to allow them to decide whether or not they want to buy them, and then be on their way.

If I were to try and force myself to write 5,000 words anyway, on the basis that "long posts rank higher in Google", that would likely backfire on me, because the fact is, the words in question probably wouldn't be very good ones. Well, there's only so much you can say about a single pair of shoes, after all: and only so much people will want to read about them, too.

My best advice to you, then, is to try to not to stress too much about the length of your post. Don't try to hit a particular word count, and don't try to stay within a certain limit, either. Instead, write a post that will help or inform your readers: don't waffle, and don't skimp on details, and you'll (hopefully) end up with a post which is exactly the length it should be.

HOW I PLAN MY BLOG CONTENT

Having agreed that consistency is one of the keys to successful blogging, your next task is to work out just how to achieve that. How often will you post a new article on your blog? How will you keep coming up with ideas? What are the best days to post? What do you do if you're sick, or need to take a vacation, or the new series of Game of Thrones has just started, and you can't rest until you've binge-watched it? Let's take those one at a time, shall we? (Other than the Game of Thrones one, I mean: you're on your own there...)

HOW OFTEN SHOULD YOU UPDATE YOUR BLOG?

This is a question a lot of bloggers ask themselves (and each other, for that matter), and the answer is – YET AGAIN - that there IS no right answer*: I know everyone wants there to be some kind of magic formula or "rule" stating that if you blog three times per week, and twice on a Sunday, your blog will achieve instant success, but nope, sorry, doesn't work like that.

(*Yes, I know I've been saying this a lot. It's the truth, though, and better I tell you the truth than try to convince you I have all the answers...)

There is, however, a very simple "secret" to knowing how often you should update your blog, and it's not really a secret, because I'm going to share it with you now:

You should update your blog as often as you can without compromising the quality of your posts.
And it's as simple as that.

I arrived at this conclusion after observing two facts about blogging:

1. The more often you post, the higher your traffic will be.

This stands to reason, because the more frequently you publish a new blog post the more content there is for people to read. The more content there is for people to read, the more often they'll come back to read it, and the more they'll potentially want to share it. Additionally, the more content there is on your blog, the more content there is to be indexed by Google, and the greater the chance of people finding it. So it's all good, right?

Well, not really. Because this brings me to my second fact:

2. Poor quality content will do your blog more harm than good.

As soon as people realise that posting more often brings them more visitors, they start to put pressure on themselves to post as often as is humanly possible: and ideally even MORE than is humanly possible. Look, we've all been there: we see the stats start to go up, so we think, "Awesome! If publishing three times a week gives me THIS much traffic, just imagine how much traffic I'll get if I post SEVEN times a week!" For this reason, daily posting has become something of a "holy grail" for many bloggers, but the fact is, daily posting (or ANY kind of strict publishing schedule) will only work if you're able to keep the quality as consistent as your schedule is.

Not everyone is able to do this. For many of us, the pressure to post as often as possible results in us rushing out content that just isn't up to our usual standard: we get so caught up in the idea that we HAVE to have a new post live by four o'clock tomorrow that we're willing to publish any old rubbish, just as long as it's SOMETHING. And that doesn't work, because poor quality content DOESN'T keep people coming back to your blog, does it? No, it makes them unsubscribe all together, and then where will you be? Probably back in that job you hated, or busy digging yourself a giant pit of despair, that's where.

So you should update your blog as often as you can, without compromising the quality. For some people that might mean posting every day, while for others it could mean posting once a week: the only real "rule" here is that, whatever your publishing schedule, you try to make it consistent. By that I don't mean that you must post a new article every Wednesday at 9pm on the dot, OR ELSE: I just mean you should avoid very long gaps between posts, or your readers will forget about you, your traffic will start to tail off, and you'll be back to digging that pit of despair. (I've been there, and I ended up with a REALLY big pit: I'm still filling it in now, actually...)

WHEN SHOULD YOU POST ON YOUR BLOG?

Just as the answer to the "how often should you post to your blog" question will differ from person to person, the question of WHEN to post will differ, too. You'll see lots of articles around the internet claiming to tell you which days of the week will get you the most traffic, and even what time of DAY you should be posting, but I'm going to save you some time by telling you to ignore them all, and EXPERIMENT.

In my case, for instance, I get the most visitors to my blog on Mondays and Wednesdays, with Saturdays being the lowest day for traffic, regardless of whether I've published a new post or not. I know this because I've experimented: I've tried updating my blog on different days, and at different times, and then I've sat down and looked at the stats, to decide what works best for me. Some trends are probably universal ones (Most bloggers report very low traffic on Christmas day, and other public holidays, for instance), but others will depend on your blog, your niche, and your readers, and only you will know what they are. So go find out.

HOW TO BLOG CONSISTENTLY

Here are some things I do to help keep my content consistent: because, as I keep on saying, consistency is key...

1. Use categories to plan content

In Wordpress, and most other blog platforms, you can organise your content by assigning each post to a "category", which is created by you. You'll probably set up your main categories during the process of creating your blog, but you can add new ones along the way, and as well as being a handy way to keep your blog organised (When a reader clicks on the link to a particular category, they'll see a list of all of the posts you've published on that topic), they can also be a useful tool when it comes to planning your content.

My blog, for instance, is a personal or lifestyle site, and the main categories are fashion, beauty, lifestyle and blogging. Each of the posts I write falls under one of those broad categories, and although I don't force myself to stick to a very rigid schedule, I do tend to publish to certain categories on certain days: so I do a 'blogging' post every Sunday, for instance, a 'lifestyle' one every Saturday, and so on and so forth. This helps keep the content varied, and it also helps me plan ahead: if I know Wednesday is the day I write about fashion, for instance, I know I have to plan a fashion-related post for that day, so I can start thinking about that in advance.

2. Write a series

Another way some bloggers like to keep their content consistent is by publishing a series of posts on a certain topic, with the posts normally going out at on a set day. Some examples I've seen are 'Beauty Tuesdays', or 'Five Things on Friday' or something similar. What you do is obviously up to you, but this type of series can work quite well, as readers know what to expect, and will often make a point of checking out your blog on the days they know the next post in the series will be published.

3. Keep an editorial calendar

An editorial calendar is basically a fancy term for a diary or planner which you use to plan out your content. Your calendar might be an ACTUAL diary, or it might just be a document on your computer, or a note on your phone which you use to track which posts you're going to publish and when. However you do it, though, if you're serious about keeping your content consistent, I recommend starting an editorial calendar, in order to plan your posts in advance.

Of course, it's worth noting here that your editorial calendar doesn't have to be set in stone: you're not obliged to write a certain post, just because you penciled it in on a certain day. To this end, I literally "pencil" posts in - i.e. I write the post title in pencil in my calendar, so I can erase it in order to move it to a different day if necessary - or just forget about it all together if I decide the idea wasn't such a great one, after all.

4. Schedule posts in advance

Many non-bloggers work under the assumption that bloggers write their posts on the day they're published, but actually, I'm not sure I know any full-time bloggers who do this. I'm sure there are some, but for most of us, one of the best ways to be consistent is to write content in advance, and then schedule it to go live on a certain day.

Every blog platform I've used allows to you to do this easily: it's simply a matter of writing your post, entering the date and time you want it to be published on, and then sitting back and letting the blog do the rest. By using this scheduling function, you can work several days, or even weeks, in advance: not only does this avoid any last-minute panics when you realise you haven't published a new post all week, and are totally out of ideas, it also allows you to plan for holidays or sick days, too. One of the big disadvantages of any form of self-employment, blogging included, is that there's no one there to pick up the slack if you need to take some time off, and by scheduling content in advance, you give yourself some much needed breathing   space,   which   can't   be   under-valued.

6

HOW I CREATE IMAGES
FOR MY BLOG

THE IMPORTANCE OF IMAGES
AND WHERE TO FIND THEM

When I started blogging, in 2006, blogs were almost entirely text-based, with very few images.

How times have changed.

These days, the words you write are still of the utmost importance, true: but images are, too. Even blogs which aren't image based, and which don't really require a photo in order to make their point, will benefit from including at least one strong image. Why? For two reasons, really:

1. It makes the post look more visually appealing, which makes people more likely to want to read it.

2. It allows the blogger to take advantage of image-based forms of social media, like Pinterest and Instagram, both of which are good places to find readers for your blog. If you don't have any images on your blog, you're not going to get pinned - and you'll be missing out on a huge source of potential traffic.

It's not just the existence of images that matters, however: the type and quality of the images you use is also important, and it stands to reason that the better your image, the greater the benefits it'll bring to your blog.

So, where do you find these images, then?

You have two main options here: you can either take your blog photos yourself, or you can acquire them from someone else.

My own preference has always been to take my own photos whenever possible. By doing this, not only will the image be unique to you, it will also allow you to create a certain "visual identity" for your blog, with people coming to associate your style of photography with you. Of course, taking good photos for your blog is one of those things that's easier said than done, and not everyone has the time, money, or inclination to invest in it. In that case, you need to get your blog photos from somewhere else. So, where?

In answer to this, I have one very important thing to say to you:

Whatever you do, please don't steal other people's images. Ever.

Many bloggers, including a lot of professional ones, are under the impression that everything on the internet is free to use, and that all they have to do is find a photo they like, save it to their computer, and then use it on their blog. The theory here is that as long as you credit the source of the image (by either stating where you found it, or linking to the owner), it's fine for you to do this, but - and I can't stress this enough - this is totally incorrect. And not only is it incorrect, it could actually get you sued, because here's a very important point for you to read, digest, and have tattooed on your forehead, if that's what it takes:

All images are automatically copyrighted, and cannot be used without permission.

A small caveat to this: there is a "fair use" clause in US law which states that you CAN use some images without permission, as long as certain conditions apply. Now, I'm not a lawyer, and I also don't live in the US, so if you want to risk using someone's photos under the fair use clause, I'm going to leave that up to you. In the case of the vast majority of bloggers, however, who are simply looking for a nice photo to illustrate their post, the safest way to do this is by asking permission first: you have nothing to lose by doing this, and it could potentially save you a lot of money in the long-run. If you don't believe me, Google "blogger sued for copyright infringement" and read all about some of the people who thought it was OK to use a photo they found on the internet... and then received a court summons and/or a hefty fine in the mail.

My advice? Don't be that person. Just... don't.

Luckily, however, there are a growing number of websites out there which provide stock images to web publishers, and these are totally legal to use. Many of them provide images for free, while some of them will charge you per image, but here's a short list to start you off:

- Pexels.com
- Gratisography
- Pixabay
- Kaboompics
- StockSnap.io

One final word of warning: each of these sites will have different conditions under which their images can be used, so please check the terms very carefully, and make sure you're using the photos you download appropriately: your bank balance will thank you for it.

MY BLOG PHOTOGRAPHY SECRETS

Stock images are all well and good, of course, but, as with all aspects of blogging, creating your own, original content is always better (not to mention safer) than using someone else's: even if you're using it legally. One of the biggest issues with stock photos is that you're not the only one who has access to them, and once you've seen that same photo on more than a handful of blogs, you're probably going to find yourself wishing you'd just taken a photo yourself. I mean, how hard can it be, right?

Well, actually, it can be pretty darn hard, to be honest - especially if photography isn't something that comes naturally to you. It doesn't for me: seriously, I can write a 1,000 word blog post without even thinking about it (just ask my long-suffering readers...), but taking a 'quick' photo to accompany it? That can take me all the livelong day - and I still probably won't be happy with the results. Which sucks, really.

Like it or not, though (and I really DON'T like it, just in case I didn't make that clear enough), photography is now a huge part of my job as a blogger. Gone are the days when you could just sit down to write a blog post, and then publish it without any images whatsoever: I mean, sure, you CAN still do that if you really want to, but it's probably not going to get you very far. This is something a lot of bloggers really struggle with - especially the ones whose blogs are based around words, rather than photos. Fashion and beauty bloggers, for instance, are used to taking photos for their blogs, and in their case, those photos are often even more important than the words which accompany them. Well, think about it: if you're thinking about buying a dress, would you rather see one good photo of it, or read a 500 word description of it? Exactly.

Bloggers in other niches, however... well, they don't tend to attach the same importance to imagery, and can actually get quite hoity-toity at the very suggestion that it's something they should be taking seriously. "I'm a WRITER," they declare haughtily. "People come to my blog for the WORDS: that's what's important!"

OK, Jack Kerouac, you can sit back down: I'm not going to argue with the importance of The Words, the quality of which will have a huge impact on the success of your blog. Before people can start to appreciate the value of your carefully crafted words, however, you have to persuade them to actually read them, don't you? That can be trickier than you might think: people DO tend to judge books by their covers, and that goes for blogs, too: although, by "their covers" I mean "their design and images". The fact is that no matter how amazing your writing is, you still need to find a way to make it stand out, and to draw readers in. One of the ways you can do that is by accompanying The Words with The Photos: and, with that in mind, here are some of the secrets I've learned about creating images for your blog...

1. WHAT YOU DO WITH YOUR CAMERA IS MORE IMPORTANT THAN HOW MUCH YOU PAID FOR IT

When I first decided it was time to get serious about my blogging career, I went out and bought an expensive DSLR camera (It's a Nikon D7000, if you're particularly curious), a couple of almost equally-expensive lenses for it, a tripod and a remote. With this little kit, I was all set to take over the fashion blogging world, with photos Vogue would be proud of: I mean, I just couldn't fail, could I?

Folks, I could totally fail. And I did. Totally. Actually, the first photos I took with that shiny new fancypants camera were WAY worse than the ones I'd been taking with my little point-and-shoot - or even with my phone. Why? Because I didn't know how to use the camera properly. The thing about DSLRs, you see, is that they're NOT point-and-shoots. Yes, you can use them on the automatic setting if you want, but that would be a bit like buying a racecar, just to drive to the corner shop every so often. The reason people buy DSLRs is so they can take advantage of the full range of features they have to offer: but that's easier said than done.

When I started complaining about how the quality of my photos wasn't nearly as good as I'd expected it to be, a wise man (OK, it was my husband: don't tell him I called him 'wise', though, OK?) explained it to me like this: point and shoot cameras, he said, are designed to take OK photos, regardless of who's using them and what their skill level is. DSLRs, on the other hand, are capable of taking AMAZING photos - but only if you know how to use them.

These cameras aren't designed for beginners: you can't just pick one up and start firing off tons of professional-quality photos. That's not to imply that DSLRs are impossible to use, of course, or that you'll have to take a college course in order to figure them out: it just means you'll have to read the manual, maybe watch some online tutorials, and, above all, take the time to practice using your camera, until you get it just right. If you're not willing to do any of this, the photos you take won't be any better than the ones you took with your phone - trust one who knows: and who has folders full of dark, blurry photos to prove it.

2. GOOD LIGHTING IS MORE IMPORTANT THAN EITHER OF THEM

I live in Scotland. In Scotland we don't get much in the way of natural daylight - and, as if to prove my point, I'm writing this on a spring day... with snow falling outside the window. When it's not snowing, it's normally raining, and when it's not raining, it's either about to rain, or it's just stopped raining. Not ideal photography conditions, in other words. One of the golden rules of photography is to shoot in natural light as often as possible - but when you don't get much of that, taking good photos for your blog can feel like an almost impossible task.

Of course, we do get SOME sunny days here: the problem with THAT, however, is that direct sunshine isn't much better for photography purposes than the dark and gloomy days I'm more used to. Harsh light creates harsh shadows, and I quickly learned that taking photos of myself in direct sunlight creates what I affectionately (by which I mean "not at ALL affectionately") think of as 'The Voldemort Effect'. I'll just leave that one to your imagination.

So, what's a blogger to do when she needs good lighting for her photos, but there's none to be found? Well, first I'll tell you what you DON'T do: you don't take the photos anyway, and hope for the best, because you just won't get it. We've all seen blogs with photos that look like they've been taken in the middle of the night, and they're just not that great to look at, are they? If you don't have enough light for your photos, then, you have to create some: not by saying, "Let there be light!", but by either taking your photos next to a window, buying yourself a softbox/other studio lighting - or, ideally, doing both.

My house gets a lot of natural light, but even that isn't enough to let me take good photos most days, so last year I invested in two softboxes, which I now set up every time I need to take photos indoors. You can pick lighting kits up on Amazon for not too much money: I'll be honest, they're a bit of a pain to have around, because they're big, bulky, and a nuisance to move around all the time, but they allow me to take reasonably bright photos even when it's overcast outside (which it almost always IS), so I can't complain. I still DO complain, obviously, because complaining is my hobby, but I try to keep it to a minimum. Most days, at least.

3. A TRIPOD AND REMOTE WILL BE YOUR NEW BFFS

If your blog requires you to take photos of yourself, the best way to do that is to get someone else to do it for you: either a professional photographer, or a willing friend/family member.

The big problem here, of course, is that pro-photographers are expensive, and friends/family members often aren't willing to drive to your chosen photography location, and then follow you around, snapping away while you pretend to sip a coffee or hail a taxi. (Oh, don't act like you've never done it...) While many of the "big" fashion bloggers DO use professional photographers (and get amazing results because of it), this is one cost that most bloggers just can't justify.

In the absence of a pro-shutterbug or Instagram boyfriend, then, your next best option is a tripod and remote, which will allow you to take photos of yourself which aren't selfies. Some bloggers, of course, do use selfies as their primary method of taking photos for their blog, but - and I mean absolutely no offense to anyone when I say this - those bloggers tend NOT to be the ones you see getting all of those brand collaborations, and making a small fortune from their blogs. The occasional selfie is all well and good, obviously, but, for the most part, they're not the most professional photos, or the best at showing off your outfit/makeup/hair/whatever it is you're trying to illustrate.

With a tripod, however, you can either use a remote control or the self-timer mode on your camera to easily take photos of yourself. No, they might not be quite as good as photos taken by another person, but there are bloggers out there who've made an art form out of self-timer photos, and there's no reason why you shouldn't be one of them: all you need is practice, patience - oh, and a decent tripod.

4. BE AWARE OF YOUR BACKDROP

If you look at the websites or Instagram feeds of any of the most popular bloggers, you'll start to notice the same old photo backdrops popping up time and time again. Outfit photos are shot against streets of perfect white houses, products are always presented on a slab of marble... and so on and so forth. The good news is that you don't have to go out of your way to replicate the "popular" photo backdrops - in fact, it's probably a good idea NOT to just mindlessly copy everyone else, huh?

There's a reason why these types of backdrops are popular, though, and it's not just that they're pretty (although that too, obviously): it's that they provide... not a blank canvas, exactly, because many blog backdrops are interesting in their own right, but certainly a blank enough canvas to let the object being photographed be the main focal point. I'm not going to tell you where to take your photos - that's one you're going to have to work out for yourself - but I will give you the following piece of advice, which is to consider your backdrop carefully, and make sure it's not too distracting.

If you're taking outfit photos indoors, for instance, you're going to want to stand against some kind of blank wall (patterned wallpaper, photo galleries and other decorations might look awesome on your wall, but they'll distract people from your outfit, and possibly even clash with it), and make sure there's not too much clutter around you. We all have messy houses sometimes, and no one's judging you for that, but at the same time, no one really wants to see photographs of it, either, so move that pile of laundry out of the shot, pick up your kid's toys that are scattered all over the floor, and just generally try to find an area of your home that's relatively clear of clutter and distractions.

If you're shooting outdoors, meanwhile, the same rules apply: try to find a spot that's fairly quiet, so your photo doesn't have tons of curious tourists in the background, and do your best to avoid things like overflowing waste-baskets or litter-strewn paths, neither of which will look attractive.

5. EDITING IS EVERYTHING

In an ideal world, all of the photos you take would be so perfectly lit and beautifully composed that you'd be able to download them from your camera and post them straight to your blog. This isn't an ideal world, though, and even the best photographers frequently find their photos could benefit from a little bit of editing.

Now, before you go getting up onto your high horse and declaring that you'd NEVER Photoshop your photos, let me save you the trouble. I'm not suggesting that you get busy airbrushing your face, taking a few inches of your waist, or otherwise altering your appearance to make you look like Gigi

Hadid's better looking sister. No, I'm talking here about simple edits: ones that will brighten up the shot, sharpen any blurred edges, and get rid of those distracting things in the background that you didn't notice when you were taking the photo. Photoshop is not the enemy, folks: in fact, it's a pretty useful tool, especially if you're working with difficult lighting conditions, or with limited photography skills.

In my case, for instance, I have such poor light to work with that often I'll look back at outfit photos I've just taken, and realise that my dress looks a different shade on film than it does in real life. Photoshop allows me to correct that: and also to brighten the photo (so you can actually see what I'm wearing in it), and crop out that discarded Coke can that's ruining the shot. Even if your photos don't need this kind of colour correction or alteration, you should at the very least be re-sizing then to lower the file size, and cropping them so you don't end up being just a tiny spot on the horizon. Most DSLR cameras take gigantic images - files so large that if you were to print them out exactly as they came off the camera, they'd end up poster-sized, at least.

When you upload them to the blog, it will automatically create a thumbnail version which will fit inside your blog design, but it won't change the actual size of the image, which means that every time someone tries to look at it on your blog, their computer will have to download that gigantic file. That's not just bad news for your reader, who just wanted to see a photo of your new shoes: it's also bad news for the load time of your blog, which is one of the factors Google takes into account when it's deciding how to rank websites. Sites which load very slowly appear further down the search results - you don't want yours to be one of them, so re-sizing and cropping your images is pretty essential.

Of course, you don't have to use Photoshop to edit your images: there are lots of different image editing tools available, and even some online ones, which you can use for free. PicMonkey is one I've used personally, and can recommend, but type "free image editor" into Google, and then take your pick!

7

HOW I GET PEOPLE
TO READ MY BLOG

One of the most common questions I get from new bloggers is how I went about finding readers for my blog, especially back in those early days, when it was brand new, and this was all still fields.

It's a good question, and I really wish I knew how to answer it, but the truth is, I have absolutely NO IDEA how people found my blog back when it first started. I DO know I didn't actually DO anything to encourage anyone to read it - I literally just built it and expected them to come: which I know goes against everything I've said in the rest of this book, but bear in mind that this was 10 years ago, the internet was a very different place, and no one really thought this whole "blogging" thing was going to last - what else was I going to do?

The funny thing is, though, they DID come. Not in their

droves, obviously: I mean, my blog wasn't an overnight success, by any means (far from it, in fact), but I did quickly pick up a few readers, which became a few more, and then more after that. Here's how I did it...

FRIENDS AND FAMILY

I started my blog the day Terry and I booked our wedding, and my original intention was that I'd use the blog to document the whole wedding-planning process. That intention died a death as soon as I worked out that, actually, planning a wedding wasn't all that interesting to me, but by that point I'd already told my friends and family that I'd started this website about the wedding, and that they should totally take a look, if they wanted to see what we were up to.

The first and most dedicated readers of Forever Amber, then, were people who knew me in real life: so, my parents and fiancé, basically. From what I've gathered, this is actually somewhat unusual, because many new bloggers instinctively seem want to keep their blog a secret: they feel it's something private, shameful even, and they worry about judgment from real-life acquaintances who won't understand it, and might even be offended or amused by it. This is particularly true of personal bloggers, or those who write about subjects like fashion or beauty: there's a perception that writing about yourself - and, worse, publishing photos of yourself - on the internet is very self-centred, and also pretty vain: I mean, how in love with your own appearance do you have to be to want everyone on the internet to look at you every day?

There's a lot I could say about this (and have said on my blog, in fact), but for now I'm just going to cut to the chase, and advise you to build a bridge and get over it: in other words, do whatever you have to do to stop feeling like your blog is something secret and shameful, and to tell people you're writing it. While there are no doubt some legitimate reasons why someone might want to keep their blog or identity private, unless you have a real reason to fear people finding out about it (Like, you're in the witness protection program, or your family would disown you if they knew you were publishing content on the internet or something. And honestly, if either of those is the case, I'm going to gently suggest that blogging isn't the best career choice, if only because you'll spend your entire life worrying about being "found out") my best advice to you is to be open about the fact that you have a blog, and to tell people about it.

This is how many bloggers gain their first few readers: even if your friends and family aren't particularly interested in your chosen subject matter, they will probably be curious enough to at least check out your blog - and if you're lucky, they might even tell someone else about it, too. Now, if you're anything like me, you're probably cringing at the very thought of this, aren't you? You're thinking about your former boss, the man across the road, and your best friend's boyfriend's creepy uncle Sam, all pouring over your words and pictures, and seriously, how weird is that going to feel? It'll be almost like they're reading your diary, won't it?

Well, no, actually it won't: because your blog is not a diary, and the sooner you realise that, the better. Even if your blog purports to BE a diary (i.e. you're writing about your life, as if the internet was your own personal journal), it STILL isn't anything like an actual diary, because diaries ARE private. They're often secret. You tell them all of your deepest, darkest thoughts, and you feel like you would die if anyone ever read them.

Your blog isn't like that. Because if you've been paying attention, you know that in order for your blog to be a success, people will have to read it. You HAVE to make sure your blog is something you're happy for people to read, and that means you CAN'T fill it with your deepest, darkest secrets, and you can't keep it private. If that's really what you want from this, then for God's sake, just start an ACTUAL diary, and forget all about this blogging lark. Blogs, you see, are in the public domain. They are written for an audience. And no matter how hard you try to keep yours secret, the people who know you WILL find out about it sooner or later, and when they do, you better hope you haven't written anything that's going to upset them or get you into trouble.

In order to avoid this, it's best that you tell people about your blog before they find it themselves. And even if they don't read it, you should assume that one day they will - and that they will read every single word of it, too. By doing that, you'll not only get used to the idea of writing for an audience, you'll make sure, right from the very start, that you don't ever write anything that might one day come back to haunt you. This will be important to you: trust one who knows.

Tell people about your blog. Put the URL in your email signature, get business cards printed and hand them out to anyone who asks what you do, hire a plane and get it to write your blog name in the sky, if you need to (OK, maybe not...): just don't be shy - there's not really much point in starting a blog if you don't actually want people to read it, after all, is there?

SOCIAL MEDIA
HOW I USE TWITTER TO PROMOTE MY BLOG

Twitter isn't my favourite social network. I mean, you have to try to restrict yourself to just 140 characters per tweet and, well, you've seen the length of this book: does it LOOK like I'd be able to restrict myself to just 140 characters? Didn't think so.
Still, like it or not, Twitter IS a pretty useful tool when it comes

to driving traffic to your blog, so use it I do: and here's how I recommend doing it…

1. Choose a handle that links to your blog/ yourself.

Your Twitter handle is the name people know you by on Twitter: mine, for instance, is @foreveramber - which makes sense, because my blog name is 'Forever Amber', geddit? Using the same name on social media as you do on your blog makes it easier for people to find you, and it also helps with your branding. Unfortunately it can be easier said than done: networks like Twitter have been around for so long now that most of the good names have already been taken, which is one of the reasons you need to think carefully about what you call your blog, and try to pick something you'll be able to use on social media, too.

If that's not possible, however, you could try going for a variation on your blog name (If @foreveramber hadn't been available, for instance, I could've gone for something like @ForeverAmberUK or @ForeverAmberBlog), or on your own name. What I don't advise is choosing something that's totally different, which will just confuse people.

2. Add your blog link to your profile.

There's a handy little space for it, but you'd be amazed how many bloggers ignore it, and don't provide any way for new followers to click through to their blogs.

3. Write an interesting bio.

Think of your Twitter bio as an elevator pitch for your blog: it may be short, but it's a great opportunity to convince people to follow you, and to click through to your website, so rather than just leaving it blank, or going for the good old age/sex/location formula, spend a bit of time creating an interesting bio, that will make people want to know more.

4. Upload a cover photo.

Well, no one wants to follow that strange little egg, do they?

5. Use branding to match your blog.

As well as your profile picture, Twitter also allows you to upload a "cover photo", which people will see when they click through to your profile. Think carefully about your choice here, and try to use an image that matches the colours and branding of your blog, so there's some continuity between your blog and your social channels.

6. Tweet links to your blog posts.

Again, this sounds really obvious: if you want to use Twitter to promote your blog, you're going to have to tweet the link to it, aren't you? A lot of bloggers, however, are a little shy when it comes to self-promotion: they worry they'll look spammy or self-important if they tweet their own links all the time, but the only real alternative is to sit back and wait for other people to do it for you - and as tactics go, that's not exactly a great one, is it? Can you imagine going to your bank manager or business adviser and, when they ask how you're going to promote your business, just going, "Um, dunno: I was hoping other people would do it for me?" Nuh-uh. If you want people on Twitter to see your blog, post the link to your blog on Twitter: it's as simple as that.

I tweet the link to each new post as soon as it's published, and then every few hours after that for the first day. I also use a Wordpress plugin called 'Revive Old Post' to automatically tweet links to my older posts at set intervals. This means there's always a link to my blog on my Twitter account, so there's always a chance of someone clicking through. Some people consider it a big "no no" to tweet a link to the same post more than once, but the fact is, Twitter moves fast, and only a small percentage of your followers will be online at any given time. If you only tweet each post once, most of your followers will miss it altogether, and your poor post will only get a fraction of the readers it deserves. No one wants that, do they?

7. But don't ONLY tweet links to your blog posts

Of course, tweeting your own links is all well and good, but if that's ALL you're doing, chances are it WILL start to look a bit spammy, and people might unfollow you as a result. Awkward, huh? The answer is to simply mix it up a bit: rather than using Twitter purely to promote your blog, use it to interact with readers and followers, tweet links to other blogs or websites you've enjoyed, and generally be social. That IS the whole point of a social network, after all...*

*I'm just going to hold my hands up here and admit that I'm not great at taking my own advice on this. Remember when I said you have to concentrate your time on the networks that are most effective for you? Twitter isn't the network that's most effective for me - SPOILER ALERT: that would be Pinterest - so my account there is a little bit neglected. You're not me, so you can do better than that: I know you can.

8. Pin one of your best posts to the top of your profile

Did you know that Twitter allows you to "pin" a particular tweet to the top of your profile? It does, and what that means is that, rather than sinking down your timeline, and disappearing into the ether, that tweet will stay at the top of the screen, and will be the first thing someone sees when they click on your profile. For that reason, it's a good idea to pin a link to one of your best blog posts: one that really demonstrates what your blog is about, and makes people want to see more. Don't forget to change your pinned tweet every so often, though: don't just promote that one post forever!

9. Use images in your tweets

Tweets which contain photos tend to get more likes, re-tweets and clicks than ones that don't: so you know what to do!

10. Join Twitter chats

Twitter chats are organised chats on specific subjects, which take place at a set time, and use a hashtag to allow participants to see all of the tweets being posted in the chat. Chats generally have a host (or hosts) whose role it is to guide the chat, normally by posting questions, which everyone taking part then answers on their own Twitter account, using the designated hashtag. There are tons of chats you can join, on every subject under the sun (You'll find a full list of available chats here: http://twubs.com/twitter-chats),and they can be a really good way to find new friends and followers who are interested in your niche. There's often an opportunity at the end of each chat for participants to post the link to their blog, which will obviously help you promote your work.

11. Make it easy for your readers to tweet links to your blog and posts

I said it would be a mistake to just sit back and wait for your readers to promote your blog on Twitter, and I stand by that. It would also, however, be a mistake to make it difficult for people to do exactly that: sometimes when a reader has really enjoyed a particular blog post, they might want to share it on Twitter, and you can encourage them to do that by adding a "tweet this" button at the bottom of your post. Many blog themes now come with social media buttons built in, but if yours doesn't, you can either use a plugin (assuming you're on Wordpress) which will automatically add share buttons to each post, or you could add them manually. I use a plugin called SumoMe, which allows my readers to easily share my posts to a variety of different social networks, but there are tons of other plugins out there which will do the same thing.

While we're on the subject, it's also a good idea to make it easy for people to follow you on Twitter, by adding a link to your profile somewhere on your blog. Most bloggers will add links to all of the networks they use in the header, footer or sidebar of their blogs - this allows your readers to easily find and follow you: and once they're following you, they'll be much more likely to click on the links you tweet, won't they?

HOW I GET FOLLOWERS ON TWITTER

Of course, none of these tips will be much use to you if you don't have any followers, will they? Many of the people you'll encounter as a blogger will encourage you to believe that you "shouldn't care about the numbers" - that it's just not the done thing to be interested in increasing your follower numbers, and that you should REALLY just be blogging "for the love of it", without any thought as to whether people are reading what you have to say.

I don't really have to tell you how ridiculous that is, do I?

Let me quickly caveat that statement: it's obviously not ridiculous to blog purely "for the love of it" if that's truly the only reason you're doing it - because you love it. Given that you're reading this book, however, I'm going to guess that you're not JUST blogging for "love", are you? It's OK, you can admit it to me: I won't judge you. Well, it would be pretty hypocritical of me, given that I freely admit to being the type of cold-hearted capitalist who blogs for money, rather than just "love".

I'm exaggerating just a little, obviously. I DO love what I do - so much so that if I became a millionaire overnight, and no longer had to work to pay the bills (and buy the shoes), I'd probably continue to blog, albeit not on the same schedule I do now. Blogging, however, is first and foremost a business for me: and if you want it to be a business for you, too, you DO need to care about "the numbers".

WHY DOES IT MATTER HOW MANY FOLLOWERS YOU HAVE ON SOCIAL MEDIA?

Two reasons:

1. The more followers you have, the more people there are to click on the links to your blog posts, and then read them.

2. Follower numbers are one of the things brands consider when they're deciding which bloggers they might want to work with: if you have a lot of followers, you'll be more likely to be chosen for campaigns, and will also be able to charge a higher rate for the ones you work on.

So, how do you get more followers on Twitter?

For the first few years I used the platform, I did absolutely nothing to grow my following: it honestly didn't occur to me that it might be important. (If you're thinking I was REALLY naive when I started blogging, you are absolutely right...) Actually, no, that's a lie: I did do ONE thing:

I FOLLOWED PEOPLE I WAS INTERESTED IN

When I joined Twitter, I followed my friends, and I followed the people whose blogs I read. Some of them followed me back, and some of them didn't: it didn't matter, though, because I wasn't following those people purely so they'd return the favour - I was following them because I was genuinely interested in what they had to say.

This point is incredibly important, because as you attempt to grow your following on Twitter, you'll encounter a lot of people who'll tell you the best way to get followers is to follow lots of people, in the hope that some of them will follow you back. There's some truth in this, too: if you follow a ton of people, after all, it stands to reason that some of them will follow you back, so if all you care about is increasing the number of followers that appears on your profile, go for it.

What I'm going to suggest to you, however, is that while you should definitely care about the numbers when it comes to blogging, you shouldn't JUST care about the numbers. Followers you see, are only useful to you if they actually read the things you post: so it's better to have 10 followers who click through and read every single post, than 100 followers who are just there out of politeness, or the misplaced belief that you followed them, so now they "owe" you a follow in return.

What about that second point, though: the one where I said brands see high follower numbers as a sign of influence? Let me quickly modify that statement: brands see high numbers of ENGAGED followers as a sign of influence. If you have followers who are just there for the sake of it (or, heaven forbid, because you bought them), it'll be pretty obvious: because they won't actually be engaging with your account. You might think you're fooling everyone, but trust me, you won't be - and you'll basically just be wasting your time sitting hitting that "follow" button, without there being anything in it for you.

So, how DO you increase your follower numbers on Twitter? Simple: by being the kind of person that people want to follow there.

Er, that's NOT that simple, is it? If it was, I'd have a LOT more followers than I do. Remember what I said about it not being my favourite platform? I'm no Twitter expert, then, and most of my followers are the simple result of perseverance: I've been on Twitter for a long time, basically, and I've gradually built up a following there. Many of the points in the previous section will help grow your follower numbers: so, taking part in Twitter chats, adding a "follow me on Twitter" button to your blog - that kind of thing. The times when my followers have increased quickly, however, it's almost always been down to one thing:

People re-tweeting something I've said.

When someone who has a lot of Twitter followers re-tweets you, their followers will often decide to follow you, too. When someone REALLY high profile (like a brand, say), re-tweets you, you can gain a large number of followers in a short period of time - and they'll be engaged followers, too.

It's not the "secret" anyone wants to hear, of course, but the best way to gain followers on Twitter is by creating interesting content there: and, just one word of warning for you - that's one of the main "secrets" to pretty much EVERY aspect of blogging...

HOW I USE FACEBOOK TO PROMOTE MY BLOG

I could actually sum this section up reeeally quickly: I DON'T use Facebook to promote my blog. Or, I DO... but not particularly actively. Facebook is by far my least favourite social network: not only do I get really bored with all of the inspirational quotes and endlessly regurgitated "memories" that people like to post there, the fact that the Facebook algorithm is designed to only show a tiny percentage of your friends or followers the things you share makes Facebook a bit of a non-starter to me. Why would I spend time sharing content on Facebook, after all, when hardly anyone will see it?

Whether you like Facebook or not, however, the fact remains that it is still a popular network, and it does still send visitors to blogs. I have far fewer followers there than I do on any other network, purely because I'm not willing to invest a lot of time in it, but here are some things I have done to promote my blog on Facebook, and which I recommend you try, too:

1. Create a Facebook fan page for your blog.

You probably already have a personal Facebook account, which you use to connect with friends, but while sharing links to your blog there will certainly get you some traffic to it, you'll be able to reach far more people if you create a "fan page" dedicated to your blog. If the word "fan page" is making you cringe a little, don't - this is just a page dedicated to your blog, which people can use to follow you on Facebook, without you having to "friend" them through your personal profile.

When Facebook first became popular, I accepted friend requests there from anyone who sent me one, which meant I ended up being "friends" with a lot of people who read my blog, but who didn't actually know me. These days, I'm a lot more careful about who I become friends with on Facebook: I might blog about my life, but I still prefer to keep some things private, so I use my personal account to chat to real-life friends, and have a "fan" page for my blog, where I post links to new posts, and interact with readers. You'll need to have a personal account to start a fan page, but the set-up process is pretty straightforward, and once you have your page up and running, you'll have a new way to connect with existing readers, and find new ones.

2. Follow the same branding rules you used for Twitter

As with your Twitter account, you're going to want to make sure your Facebook page has the same name as your blog, uses the same profile picture, and has the same kind of branding.

3. Post links to your blog posts.

Capt'n obvious, reporting for duty once again! As with Twitter, if you want to use Facebook to promote your blog, you have to ... promote your blog. It's possibly a little easier to get over the feeling of being a spammer on Facebook, because as you've created a page specifically for your readers to follow, you at least know they're there because they WANT to see links to your blog, and expect you to post exactly that. If you're using Wordpress, there are plugins you can use which will automatically post a link to each new blog post to your Facebook page (I use Jetpack, but there are tons of others which do the same thing), or you can choose to do it manually: however you choose to do it, however, you MUST do it: because it's not like people will find links to your blog posts on Facebook if they're not there to start with, is it?

4. Don't ONLY post links to your blog posts

Although the purpose of a blog Facebook page is to allow people to follow you on their preferred network, there's evidence to suggest that if you ONLY post links to your own posts, fewer people will see them. This is because of the Facebook algorithm, which ranks content according to popularity: so, the more popular your Facebook post is (i.e. the more "likes" and comments it gets), the more people Facebook will show it to in their newsfeeds.

This is bad news for us bloggers, because it means that not everyone who follows your page will actually get to see your content: in fact, sometimes only a tiny percentage of your followers will be shown the link to that amazing new blog post you just spent hours slaving over. Facebook, much like God himself, works in mysterious ways, but the basic rule here is that the more interaction your updates get, the more people Facebook will show those updates to. So, it's a bit of a Catch-22, really: you need people to interact with your page in order for them to see updates from it in their newsfeeds, but people can't interact with it if they don't ever see it. Confused? You will be.

The only way to break out of this vicious circle is to encourage more people to interact with your updates. There are various ways to do this: for instance, you could try asking a question, posting a link to an interesting news article or funny blog post: hell, you could even post one of those inspirational quotes everyone seems to love so much, or a "hilarious" video or article. ("You'll never guess what happened next!") The key here is to experiment, and to pay close attention to what works, and what doesn't: oh, and if you're thinking that posting other people's content on your Facebook page is a waste of time, because it won't send visitors to YOUR blog, remember that the more interaction you get on the page as a whole, the more likely Facebook will be to show your content (including links to your blog posts) to more of your followers.

A quick word on Facebook advertising
One of the ways Facebook makes money is by offering users

the opportunity to pay to "boost" the posts they publish there. So, if you post a link to your latest blog post, say, and Facebook only shows it to 5% of your followers, you can pay to have it shown to more of them. Prices vary for this, but generally start from £2 - £3, so it's not hugely expensive.

Is it worth it, though?

In my experience, not really: I've paid to boost posts a few times, and although it has resulted in more interaction on the boosted posts themselves, I can't say I've noticed much of an effect on the number of people who click through to my blog from them. The other thing worth bearing in mind here is that you can pay to boost one post, but that won't help the next post you publish, or the one after that: so unless you want to pay to boost ALL of them, you might not feel it's worth your while.

HOW I GOT HALF A MILLION
FOLLOWERS ON PINTEREST

Unlike Twitter, Pinterest is the kind of social network where you don't necessarily need a lot of followers in order to get some good traffic from it: all you need is for one influential pinner to re-pin one of your images, and you can stand to gain a lot of referrals from it - and for a long time, too.

With that said, it stands to reason that the more followers you have, the greater the chances of people re-pinning your content: so here's the secret of how I got myself over half a million Pinterest followers - a figure which far outstrips all of my other social networks, and still has me pinching myself in disbelief every time I try to picture them all in a room together.

I give you fair warning here: this particular secret is probably going to disappoint you, because, as with so much else in this wonderful blogging world of ours, it's not like you can just push a button or say a magic word, and BOOM! Half a million followers! (Well, actually, you CAN - it's called buying followers and it's NOT recommended.) So here it is:

I got featured by Pinterest.

There I was, minding my business, with just a couple of thousand followers, and absolutely no idea how to best use Pinterest to grow my blog. I mean, I was so in the dark about it that I wasn't even pinning my own content: I thought that was a big "no no", and just really spammy, so I'd dip in and out every now and then, pin a few things, then leave.

Then, one day, I got an email from Pinterest's UK team, asking me if I'd like to be a "featured user": ever notice those "you might like to follow" suggestions that sometimes pop up in the corner of your Pinterest screen? They asked if I'd like to be one of those suggestions. So I said no, obviously: I mean, why would I want thousands of new followers, and the opportunity to have my content circulated widely on one of the biggest social networks of the moment? Pshaw! Not me, I was happy just to soldier along in my modest little fashion, and... OK, ya got me: OF COURSE I said yes. In fact, I couldn't say 'yes' fast enough - they basically sent me the email, and it went a bit like this:

PINTEREST PERSON: *Hi Amber, we were wondering if you'd like to be a featured user on...*

ME: *YES! WHERE DO I SIGN UP?*

A few days later, I got another email to say they'd added me to the 'suggested users' list, and overnight my follower numbers skyrocketed. I was gaining thousands of new followers every day - and this went on for six months, which was the length of time they'd agreed to promote me for. By the end of that 6 month period, I had half a million followers: sure, the growth slowed down - waaaaaayy down - as soon as Pinterest stopped promoting my profile, but I didn't think I could complain too much. This was probably the luckiest break I ever got as a blogger, and the kind of promotion I couldn't have paid for: so I was very, very grateful for it.

Now, I know what you're thinking: "Well, la-di-dah! Good for you, Amber - but I should be so lucky as to have something like that happen to ME!"

So, I have two things to say to that:

1. It's good that you recognise there's sometimes an element of luck involved in blogging. Remember way back at the start of this book, back when dinosaurs still roamed the earth, and I told you that many of the "big" bloggers out there got where they are through a combination of luck and good timing? I didn't say that just to meet the word-count: I said it because it's true, and luck is the one thing you can't count on and replicate. With that said, though...

2. You COULD be that lucky. Yes you could. Because it wasn't JUST down to luck at all.
Want to know why Pinterest approached me with the offer to make me a featured user? They didn't just do it from the goodness of their hearts, did they? No, what they told me was that they'd taken a look at my account, and they really liked some of my boards - specifically some of the fashion-related ones. This came as something of a surprise to me, because, like I said, I wasn't a huge Pinterest user at that time, and I definitely wasn't one of those people who disappears down the Pinterest rabbit hole for days at a time, finally emerging blinking into the light, clutching a blanket scarf and a Starbucks cup. Nuh-uh. It seems that what I WAS pinning, however, was exactly the kind of thing the Pinterest team WANTED users

to pin, and that was - drumroll, please -

Original content, pinned directly from the source.

Because I didn't have the time to spend hours re-pinning other people's images, I'd been using Pinterest primarily as way to organise and keep track of the things I found online and knew I might want to find again someday. In other words, I was using Pinterest in exactly the way it was always intended to be used: I wasn't trying to promote myself, I wasn't trying to sell anything... I was just using the platform in a way that I found useful.

And THAT'S what got their attention.

Pinterest thrives on re-pins, but what it REALLY wants is original content: images pinned directly from the website you found them on, and which have never appeared on the platform before. That's exactly the kind of stuff I was pinning, so I guess you could say the REAL secret to my half a million Pinterest followers is the same old secret I keep banging on about:

Create great content.

Don't think about selling, or promoting, or doing ANYTHING other than creating something that's useful - either to yourself, or to someone else. That's what got my account noticed by Pinterest, and that's what got me from 2,000 followers to 500,000 followers in the space of just 6 months.

What did I DO with those 500,000 followers, though? That's a good question: let's look at it in more detail...

AMBER McNAUGHT

HOW I USED PINTEREST TO RAPIDLY
GROW MY BLOG TRAFFIC

By the middle of 2015, I had 500,000 Pinterest followers... but I wasn't getting a huge amount of traffic from the site. Remember how I said Pinterest is the kind of network where you don't really NEED a ton of followers to get great traffic from it? It's also the type of network where you can HAVE a ton of followers, and get very little return from them - which is what happened to me.

I was super-confused, and pretty disappointed with this state of affairs. When Pinterest had first offered to feature me, I'd assumed I was set for life - that it would send me so much traffic my site would probably crash: which is every blogger's dream, really, isn't it?

Well, needless to say, that didn't happen. Actually, nothing much happened for a very long time. And as my Pinterest followers grew, but my blog traffic remained exactly the same, I grew more and more despondent. Then the penny dropped. I can't remember exactly HOW it dropped - I think I'd maybe been reading one of the Facebook blogger groups I was a member of, and someone had been talking about how she used Pinterest to grow her blog traffic - but all of a sudden, the answer was crystal clear:
I wasn't getting traffic from Pinterest, because I wasn't adding my blog posts to Pinterest.

I mean, talk about a D'UH moment. Seriously: why would I expect people to click through from Pinterest to my blog, when there was nothing there to click through FROM? Or not much, anyway: some of my blog posts had been pinned by kind-hearted readers, but most of them didn't appear on Pinterest at all - because I hadn't put them there. I'd been basically waiting for the mountain to come to me, hadn't I? I thought it would be "spammy" to pin my own posts, so I was just sitting there twiddling my thumbs, hoping other people would do the hard work for me. Of course, that wasn't happening (or not often enough to make a difference), and as blog tactics go, "hoping" isn't really a great one, is it? So I decided to take things into my own hands. Here's what I did...

1. CREATED A FEW PINTEREST BOARDS BASED AROUND CATEGORIES COVERED IN MY BLOG.

So I had one for "outfits", one for "lifestyle", one for "travel", and so on.

2. STARTED PINNING MY OWN CONTENT TO THOSE BOARDS.

Every day, I'd spend a bit of time going through my blog, and pinning photos to the boards I'd created. What I quickly realised was that adding a pin to Pinterest is a bit like posting a link on Twitter: as soon as you do it, people who are on the network at the time will see it, and will click on it, through sheer curiosity. This creates an instant surge of traffic - and I created lots of those little traffic surges, by pinning multiple times a day. Once I'd run out of things to pin, I did one of two things:

a. I modified the images on older posts, and then pinned them.

Many of my older blog posts either didn't have images in them at all (the horror!), or had images which were grainy, dull, and just not compelling enough to make people want to click on them. So, every day I'd go through my blog's archive, update the images that needed it, and then pin them. As for the images that didn't need to be updated, meanwhile...

b. I just pinned them again: sometimes to a different board, sometimes to the same one as before.

A lot of people think that you should only pin a particular image once: I disagree, though. As with Twitter, if you only pin your images once, people will only have the opportunity to see them once: and you'll only get traffic from them once. Not really fair, is it? The answer is to pin your content more than once... but to space it out appropriately, so you're not just re-pinning the same old image, day after day. To help with this, I also...

3. SIGNED UP TO A PIN SCHEDULING SITE

One of the problems with pinning from your own site is that if you do it too much, it DOES start to look spammy, and to annoy people. Rather than flooding people's Pinterest feeds with thousands of photos of your shoes, then, it's better to spread them out over the course of a day - or even a few days. Who has time for THAT, though, I hear you ask? Well, you do, actually: because the next step is to use a Pin Scheduler, which allows you to select pins which the service you're using will then post to Pinterest on your behalf, leaving a decent interval between each one.

To do this, I used a service called Boardbooster: it costs a few dollars per month, but I figured it was worth it, because, as well as scheduling new pins, Boardbooster also has a service they call "looping", where pins from a selected board are re-pinned to the same board, meaning that they'll appear in people's newsfeeds again. I enabled this service, too, and the combination of this, plus everything I've said above, had a quite startling effect: in the space of just a few months, my traffic from Pinterest grew rapidly, and because of that, so did the traffic to my blog, which, by the end of that year, had exceeded 150,000 pageviews per month, for the first time ever.

It was a pretty good Christmas gift, all things considered.

The traffic continued to grow up until March 2016, when Pinterest suddenly decided to change its algorithm. Overnight, my referrals from the site started to drop and while I still get a healthy amount of traffic from Pinterest, this is a good lesson on why you should never rely on just one source of traffic. Because that would be silly now, wouldn't it? With that said, if you do want to try to use Pinterest to grow your blog, here are some other tips for you:

Create Pinworthy images

Well, D'UH! It's one of those "Goes without saying" pieces of advice, but images have never been more important in blogging, and it stands to reason that if you want people to pin your images, you need to provide great images for them to pin. If you're a fashion or beauty blogger, your photos have to be the best they can possibly be – so go back to the chapter on taking blog photos, and learn it by heart.

If your blog relies mostly on text, rather than on photos, meanwhile, you can still get traffic from Pinterest by creating graphics to illustrate your posts. I like Canva for creating blog graphics, but there are lots of other (free) programs out there which will let you create graphics without having to know much about design. Don't make the mistake of thinking your blog post doesn't really need an image: it might not require a photo to get the point across, but if you don't have any images on it, people can't pin it, so unless you're actively trying to prevent people reading those precious words of yours, get snapping!

Make it easy for people to pin

People like to pin, but they don't like to have to hunt around to work out how to do it. Adding the 'Pin It' button to your images will increase your chances of being pinned.

Use vertical images where possible

The taller the image, the more it will stand out on Pinterest, and the more likely it will be to get re-pinned – so use tall images rather than square ones.

Pin your own photos

I talked at length about this above, so I won't repeat myself: just do it. You know it makes sense.

Describe your pins

I think a lot of people – myself included – have a habit of simply hitting the "Pin It" or "repin" button, and then pinning the image with whatever text was already in the description box. It's quicker and easier to pin that way, but you get more re-pins and click-throughs if you actually take the time to write a short description of the pin, and why you're saving it – using relevant keywords helps, too.

Verify your account

Verifying your Pinterest account involves adding a piece of code to your template to allow Pinterest to verify that the blog is yours. By doing this, you get your blog link next to the name in your profile, so people who follow you can click through to your site: you'll find the option to verify your account, plus instructions how to do it, by clicking the "settings" icon.

Check what other people are pinning from your site

Pinterest Analytics gives you fairly in-depth information on what people are pinning from your site, but you can also see all of your most recent re-pins at a glance by typing pinterest.com/source/YOURDOMAIN into your browser. (Er, obviously replace "YOURDOMAIN" with your ACTUAL domain...) As well as it being interesting to see what's caught people's attention, this also helps you learn what works and what doesn't. And, of course, once you know what works, you also know what to keep on doing!

Use Rich Pins

Rich Pins are pins which contain extra information: they're more useful to pinners, and are more visible in the Pinterest search results. There's a guide on the Pinterest website which explains how to sign up and use them: it's a little bit tricky, but definitely worth doing!

A QUICK WORD ON INSTAGRAM

Back at the start of this section, I mentioned the "big four" of social media, by which I was referring to:

TWITTER
FACEBOOK
PINTEREST
and
INSTAGRAM

These are the four networks I use most, but they don't all send traffic to my site. Instagram, for instance, is by far my favourite of the four (Shh! Don't tell the others: Twitter in particular gets really jealous...), but I don't find that it sends a huge amount of traffic to my blog. This won't be true for all bloggers, of course, but my experience is that people who use Instagram prefer to remain on Instagram: because there's no easy way to click through from an Instagram photo to a blog (You can put your URL in your Instagram profile, but not in the caption of your images), most people just won't bother - so you can have a lot of followers there, but not see a huge increase in the visitors to your blog.

With that said, Instagram is still an important network for bloggers, particularly those in the fashion and lifestyle fields, who will often be able to turn their large Instagram following into cold, hard cash, by accepting Instagram-based sponsorships: i.e. brands will literally pay them just to post a photo on Instagram. Kind of makes you wonder why you're even bothering with this whole "blogging" thing, huh?

Now, my own Instagram following isn't nearly large enough for that to be happening on any kind of regular basis: I do get the occasional Insta-centric sponsorship, but not often enough to make a living from it, the way some people do. In my case, then, I use Instagram mostly to build my "brand" (Yup, I went there: I referred to myself as a "brand". I am so very sorry.), by offering my followers "behind the scenes" looks at my life and previews of upcoming posts. I also post a photo from each new blog post I publish on my Instagram account, with a caption inviting people to click through and read it, but it's mostly a place to build community, and get to know my readers a little better.

With that in mind, I have only one real Instagram "secret" to share:

You have to post amazing images.

If you think that's too obvious for words, then you obviously haven't seen the hundreds of bad photos people post to Instagram: the inspirational quotes (Seriously, would people just cool it with the inspirational quotes already?!); the photo taken at a rock concert, depicting a tiny dot of a person, on a far-away stage; the endless, blurry selfies; the list goes on.

Instagram is a photo-sharing site, but you sometimes wouldn't know that to look at it. Many people use it purely to document their lives, and don't give a second's thought to the quality of the photos they post there. That's a totally valid way to use Instagram, by the way - IF you're a hobby blogger, or casual user. If you're looking to blog professionally, however, and hope to use Instagram to help you with that, you HAVE to post your very best photos - and only your very best photos.

As with Twitter, I get most "likes" and follows on Instagram when I post my best work, and when someone more popular than me re-grams something I've posted. People only re-gram high-quality images - and they only LIKE high-quality images, too. So use Instagram to build your community, offer another advertising opportunity, or drive traffic to your blog - and do it by posting amazing photos, that people will genuinely want to share.

Before I started blogging, I was a member of a couple of large forums aimed at women in their 20s and 30s. Although I was never a particularly prolific poster, when I started my blog, I added a link to it to my forum signature, and found I got quite a few new readers from it. One of the people who clicked through from a forum happened to have a blog of her own, which she linked to mine from, and I got a few more regular readers from there.

The key to using forums is to BE COOL. By that I mean you can't just go riding into someone's forum and start spamming your blog link everywhere, because that'll do you more harm than good. Instead, just continue to post as you would if you didn't have a blog to promote: be helpful, friendly and, above all, NORMAL, and make sure your URL is in your signature, where people can see it. You'll be much more likely to get new readers by being yourself than by desperately trying to force people to click so relax, people, relax...

If forums aren't for you, or you just can't find one relevant to your niche, Facebook groups are another place to connect with like-minded people, and they can also be a great source of traffic to your blog. You'll find groups on every subject under the sun: there are dozens dedicated to blogging, for instance, and they can be an excellent source of information, advice and sheer solidarity, quite apart from anything else. By searching for groups related to the topics you write about, however, you'll be able to put your content in front of people who are genuinely interested in it: as with the advice on forums, however, just be careful not to spam, and read the rules of the groups you're joining, rather than simply dumping your link and running.

As with forums, groups will work best when you use them for the purpose they were designed for: to communicate with other people. No one likes a spammer, so join in, enjoy the conversation, and only reference your blog when it's appropriate to do so. Wondering how you'll know? You'll know. Because you're human, and you probably don't like spammers either, do you? If you wouldn't like it if someone else did it, chances are other people won't want YOU doing it either: simple.

Want to know what one of the biggest sources of traffic to my blog is? Wait: why am I asking that? It's not like you'd be reading this for some other reason is it? Well, I'll tell you what you want to know: one of the biggest sources of my blog's traffic is...

Other blogs.

Yup, people who read my blog, and then decide to link to it for some reason. Sometimes that link comes from a blogroll (a list of blogs the person reads), other times it might be part of a post they've written, maybe rounding up their favourite outfits of the week, say, or the posts they've particularly liked. If I'm REALLY lucky, someone might like my blog enough that they'll ask to interview me, or do some other kind of feature: I write these people's names on a piece of gold-backed paper, and I kiss it every night before I go to bed - THAT'S how much I love those people.

So, how do you go about persuading other bloggers to link to you? Well, you could just ask them, obviously, and some people do: I occasionally get emails from bloggers saying something like, "Hey, Amber! Want to link to my blog? I'll link back!" (Actually, sometimes they don't even offer to link back. Which is just... yeah.) I don't ever agree to do this, by the way. I know that makes me sound like a cold, hard bitch, but that's because I AM a cold, hard bitch. OK, not really: it's just because if I were to randomly link to every single blogger who asked me to, I'd have a blogroll five miles long, and no one would ever read it, because who has the time to scroll through a five mile long list of blogs? Not this girl.

The other reason I don't link to everyone who asks me - even if they offer to link to me, too - is because there really isn't much point to it. Links are most valuable to me when they come from blogs which have a similar audience to my own, and which - not to put too fine a point on it - actually HAVE an audience. A link from a motorcycle blog, for instance, isn't going to be of much use to my fashion/lifestyle blog, because any crossover in audience between that blog and my own will be pure coincidence. A link from a blog that doesn't have any readers, meanwhile, doesn't have much value to me either: sure, it would be super-nice of me to link to it anyway, just to help the new blogger out, but I'll only do that if I REALLY like them, and genuinely adore their blog. Otherwise we're back to that 5 mile blogroll, and no benefit to anyone.

So, just randomly asking bloggers to link to your website probably isn't going to work for you. Here are some things that just might, though…

Commenting

Most blogs have a comment section of some kind, and most of those comment sections have a box you can type the URL of your own blog into, so that people who read your comment can click on the link and visit your blog. As with my point about forums, the key here is to be natural about it: don't, whatever you do, leave insincere comments just so you can post your link (trust me, the bloggers you do this to will know you're doing it, and they really won't appreciate it…). Instead, comment naturally and sincerely, and remember: no one likes a spammer. If you leave a comment saying, "Great post! Read my blog!", no one's going to care enough to click through; if, however, you leave one that's interesting, which adds something to the discussion, and which doesn't sound like self-promotion, they just might.

Guest posting

Guest posts are posts written by someone other than the person who owns the blog. Some bloggers accept guest posts all year round, others only do it on an occasional basis (when they're going on vacation, for instance, and need someone to help keep their blog running), but if you can find a blog in a similar niche to your own, offering to submit a post to it can be a great way to get the word out about your blog.

Guidelines for guest posts differ from blog to blog, but generally you'll be expected to write something original (i.e. you can't simply re-post something you've already published on your own blog), which is in-keeping with the tone of the blog you're submitting it to, and to not sound too sales-y: so you can normally add your blog link to the end of the article, but you can't pepper it throughout the text, got it?

Building relationships

By far my biggest success in gaining traffic from other blogs has come simply from building relationships with other bloggers. As with most of the things I've tried, this came about completely by accident: I like blogs, so I obviously READ blogs, and by doing that, and leaving comments on them, I gradually became friends with some of their authors, who would link to my site occasionally, or add me to their blogroll. I should say here that I didn't start building these friendships with the aim of growing my blog traffic from them, and you shouldn't either: you should make friends with other bloggers because you like them, and because it's good to have friends who know what you're talking about when you need someone to vent to about blogging. Just think of any additional readers they send your way as an added bonus...

As with the subject of social media, I could devote several chapters to search engine optimisation, and still only scratch the surface, but, in very simple terms, search engine optimisation is the art of making sure your blog appears in the results page of search engines like Google when someone searches for a topic you've written about. Obviously the higher up the page you appear, the more visitors to your site you'll get, so this can yield amazing results if done right.

In this age of social media, a lot of bloggers - particularly fashion and lifestyle bloggers - think they don't need to bother about SEO, and that social media alone will be enough to drive traffic to their blog. There is some degree of truth in that: SEO is no longer the be-all-and-end-all of the Internet, and there are plenty of blogs out there which owe most of their traffic to Pinterest or Twitter. To ignore SEO altogether, however, is to miss an important trick, because not only are the readers who arrive from a search engine highly targeted (they searched specifically for the information you're offering, so they're likely to read the post they find themselves on), these are also the readers who are most likely to click on your adverts, if you have any. Ranking highly on a search engine for a particular term also means you'll get traffic from that result for years - long after Twitter and Facebook have stopped sending readers to your latest post, the search engine traffic will keep on coming, and the more of it you can attract, the better.

The problem, of course, is that if search engine optimization is an art, it's a pretty dark one, and no one really knows how EXACTLY to make sure your site will rank well in Google et al. There are plenty of theories, and many of them are very sound ones too, but Google, for instance, changes its algorithm frequently, and what works one month might not work the next, so it's important to try to keep up with developments in the field. With that said, the absolute basics are pretty straightforward, and in order to understand how to make sure your blog posts show up in search engines, it's useful to think of the internet as a giant library: which is what it IS, when you really think of it.

If the internet is a library, then, your blog is just one of the millions and millions of books sitting there on the shelves, waiting for someone to come and pick it up. How does that happen, though? How do you persuade that casual browser to choose YOUR book, rather than one of the thousands of others like it? As I said, there are lots of things you COULD do, but probably the most important one is to find out what, exactly, that person is looking for. If they're looking for a book on frogs, and yours is about tigers, they're obviously never going to read it, no matter WHAT do you do, so your first task when it comes to optimising your blog is to find out what people want to know about your chosen topic: what do they type into Google, that could lead them to your site?

Working this out is known as keyword research, and there are a number of handy tools on the internet itself to help you do it. Google's own Keyword Tool is perhaps the best known: it allows you to type in a particular search term, and find out how many people are searching for it, and it'll also give you suggestions of related phrases that might ALSO bring traffic to your site. All YOU have to do is choose the search term you think will work best for you: this is trickier than you might think, though, because you have to bear in mind here that you're not the only blogger trying to do this. You might think it makes sense, for instance, to choose a keyword phrase that gets a million searches per day - because who WOUDLN'T want a million people per day to arrive at their blog, having searched for that term? - but the reality is that those very popular search terms will be incredibly hard to rank for, because they will, of course, be hugely competitive.

In other words, it's probably better to optimise your post for the keywords "mating habits of purple-tailed frogs in the Serengeti", say, than simply "frogs". (Actually, it's probably better not to optimise your post for EITHER of them, but you know what I mean...) Sure, there will be far fewer people searching for the first option than there will be for the second, but it's sometimes better to rank #1 on Google for a search term that gets 100 searches a day, say, than to rank #1,976 on Goggle for a phrase that gets 1,000 searches each day, right?

So, you've chosen the phrase (or phrases) you want to try to optimise your post for: what next?

Next, you go back to that library analogy, and ask yourself what you'd look for, if you were looking for that book about purple tailed frogs. What would make one book stand out above all of the others? There are a few factors which might work here: the name of the book probably being the main one. If the book you're looking for has the words "purple tailed frogs" in the title, you'll be more likely to pick it up than you would be if it DIDN'T contain those words, wouldn't you? I mean, D'UH: obviously!

You'll also be more likely to pick up a book that, as well as having a title that makes reference to those purple tailed frogs you're so interested in, ALSO contains chapter listings which use those words, wouldn't you? If it has photos of the frogs scattered through it? Even better. What does this mean for your blog post, though, I hear you ask? And when am I going to stop talking about frogs? Well, here's the thing:

The title of the book = the title of your blog post.

A lot of bloggers make the mistake of giving their posts the kind of titles they think they might see in a magazine: so, if they're writing about red shoes, say, they might call the post "Red Alert", in a bid to be all magazine-y and creative. They'd be better off just calling it "red shoes", though - or something that at least mentions those words - because the fact is, Google may be super-bright, but it's also kind of stupid. If you call your post, "Red Alert", it won't know that it's ACTUALLY about shoes - so when someone types "red shoes" into the search box, Google won't suggest your post to them as an option.

The photos in the book = the images in your post

It makes sense that if you're writing about red shoes (just to continue with the shoe metaphor, and get away from the frog one, because that was starting to get weird), you'd want to include some photos of red shoes, wouldn't you? Here's the thing, though: the people who read your post will obviously be able to see that the images you've included do, indeed, depict red shoes. Search engine optimisation, however, is about getting SEARCH ENGINES to look at your post and work out what it's about, and that's where you have to once again remember that Google is clever... but not THAT clever. Google, for instance, doesn't know what photos show. It knows that there IS a photo in your blog post, but it doesn't know what the image depicts: unless you tell it.

You do this by using what's called an "alt tag": a piece of code which is attached to your image, and allows search engines to work out what the image shows. Most blog editors will allow you to add this alt tag when you add the image: in Wordpress, for instance, when you hit the "add media" button and upload an image, there's a space for the image title, one for the caption, and one for the "alt tag". Many new bloggers completely ignore all of these boxes, which means their images all have names like, "DMC65797-87". What's a "DMC65797-87"? I have no idea, and neither does Google, so by simply changing that name to "red shoes", and using an alt tag which ALSO contains those words, you're able to make it crystal clear what that photo is of, and Google will thank you for it. (Well, actually, it won't: Google is kind of stand-offish, to be honest. It'll at least know how to rank your post better, though, and that's the main thing.)

The chapter headings in the book = the sub-headings in your blog post

If your blog post is relatively short, you might not need to use sub-headings. Longer posts, however, can really benefit from being broken up into sections, with each one given its own heading: this not only helps readers know what the post is about, it helps Google, too.

How does Google know a line of text is a sub-heading, and not just, well, a line of text, I hear you ask? Good question: and, as with the images, it knows because you tell it, by adding a header code to the HTML of your post: so the title up above, for instance, might look like this:

<h1> The chapter headings in the book = the sub-headings in your blog post.</h1>

The contents of the angle brackets tell your blog how you want this line of text to look - and they also tell Google and other search engines that this is a heading, not simply a line of text. If you're thinking that sounds technical, don't: most blog themes will have a stylesheet with sub-headings already built into them, so all you have to do is select the text you want to highlight, and select the relevant option from the drop-down menu: it'll take you seconds, but will help the way your blog performs in search engines forever.

The text of the book = the text of your blog post

This is another one from the "so obvious it goes without saying" files, but if you want your blog post to rank in Google for a particular set of keywords, you're probably going to have to use those words at least SOMEWHERE in your post, huh?

The bibliography in the book = the links in your post

Finally, if you're looking for even more information on your chosen subject than one book could possibly give you, you might flick to the bibliography, to see what else you can read on the topic. In the case of your blog post, the "bibliography" would be the links within the post - and no, you don't have to put them all at the end, like in a real book. When it's ranking websites, Google sees outbound links as a good sign (for the most part), because a post which contains links to MORE information will presumably be more useful to the reader than one that doesn't. By linking to related articles, then, you're telling search engines that your post is a real mine of information - and who WOUDLN'T want to read it?

It's not quite that easy, though.

I should say at this point that all of this is vastly, VASTLY over-simplifying the complex topic of search engine optimization. For instance, you could follow all of the instructions in this chapter to the letter, and STILL not get your post to rank well on Google, because think about it:

would YOU want to read a book called 'Purple Tailed Frogs', in which every single chapter was called 'Purple Tailed Frogs', and when you scanned through the text, all you could see was the words 'Purple Tailed Frogs', repeated over and over again? Probably not: because that book sounds dull as hell, doesn't it? It also sounds like it was probably written by some kind of robot, and therein lies the problem: if you just stuff your blog post full of the keyword you want to rank for, you're going to make it sound REALLY un-natural, and Google doesn't like that. (Google doesn't like a lot of things. You'll find that out.)

Ultimately, then, you have to remember that you're writing for humans, not search engines. The aim of any search engine is to provide its users with the most useful and relevant article for the search term they type in. So while it obviously helps to be aware of all of the points above, and to remember that you're never going to rank for a keyword term if you don't ever use it, there's really only one thing you have to know about search engine optimisation:

You have to write useful content.

And that's it, really. Think about what YOU would find useful if you were the person searching the library for that book. Then write that.

I should really have put that part first, shouldn't I?

AMBER McNAUGHT

8

HOW I MAKE MONEY
FROM MY BLOG

WHEN SHOULD YOU MONETISE YOUR BLOG?

If you've been following my advice, by this point you should have a blog and a readership: there's only one other thing you need in order to make a living from blogging, and it's the thing no one really likes to talk about:

MONEY

So, let's talk about money. It is, after all, the reason you bought this book, so you're probably wondering why it's taken us so long to get to it, aren't you?

Well, yes, you're right: it took a bit of time, but as I said in the last chapter, before you can make money from blogging, you need to have:

A) a blog

and

B) lots of people who read it

This is the reason I've put monetisation at the end of this book, rather than at the start. It's not that I don't think you should start a blog with the aim of making money from it: quite the contrary, in fact. Back at the start of this book (hey, remember the start of this book? Seems like a long time ago now, doesn't it?) I talked about how, for those who want to make it a career, starting a blog is no different from starting a magazine. It's a business, in other words, and now we've reached the "business" part of it.

So, when should you start to monetise your blog?

This is the question every new blogger wants to know the answer to, but it can be hard to know when the right time is. The fact is, some bloggers make a healthy living from 20,000 visitors per month, while others can have ten times that amount, and STILL not make enough to go full-time. Complicated, huh?

As there's no "right" answer to the "when to monetise" question, then, I'm simply going to tell you which methods I've used personally, and how. I'm also going to give you what I think is the most important piece of advice on this subject, which is this:

Diversify your income streams.

Don't just rely on one source of monetisation if you want to make a living from blogging. Doing that might make you some money, sure, but it's incredibly risky, because if that income stream dries up (and it could), you'll be back to square one before you know it. Like most bloggers, I use multiple monetisation techniques, some of which you can start using right away, and others which you might want to wait a while before trying.

In my case, although I had absolutely no idea of the potential blogging could have when I started back in 2006, it was always my intention to make at least SOME money from my site, so I incorporated some advertising into the design right from the very start. I made very little money from it, of course (you DO need at least SOME traffic to make money from advertising, and a brand new blog doesn't normally have that), but if it's your aim to make a living from selling advertising on your blog, it's still something I'd recommend, for the following reasons:

1. It allows you to incorporate the ad slots into your blog layout right from the start, rather than having to modify the design later.

2. You have the opportunity to experiment, and find out what works best for your blog. (Which might not be the same things that work best for someone else's blog...)

3. It makes your intentions clear.

This last point is an important one. There are plenty of people out there who don't think blogs should be monetised, and who feel let down, and almost betrayed when a blogger they follow suddenly starts to monetise their content. You'll never be able to change these people's minds about whether or not bloggers deserve to be paid for their work, but you can avoid a backlash from your readers by making it clear right from the very start that your blog isn't just a hobby, and that you intend to make money from it.

And here's how you can do it: or, rather, how I do it:

GOOGLE ADSENSE

I wrote a little about Google AdSense in an earlier chapter, but just to recap, it's a contextual advertising program which attempts to match the adverts displayed on your site to the things you write about: so write a post about shoes, for instance, and it'll show your readers adverts for shoes. They're presumably reading the post in the first place because they're interested in shoes, so the idea is that they click on the adverts next to the article, and each time someone clicks, you earn commission. You'll normally only earn a few cents for each click, but as advertisers essentially "bid" to appear higher up in the search results, some adverts pay more than others, and you'll also find that some topics are more profitable than others, too. So my first AdSense "Secret" is a really obvious one:

WRITE ABOUT THINGS PEOPLE CAN BUY.

I've used AdSense on all of my websites, and you might be surprised to know that the site that earns the least from Google AdSense is the site which gets the most traffic. You'd think simple mathematics would dictate that the more traffic a blog gets, the more money it'll make, but that's not necessarily the case, and what I've found is that AdSense is most effective on the blogs (or just on the blog posts) which talk about things people can buy: shoes, for instance. Or dresses. Or books. Or holidays. Or anything else that people can click on an advert and buy.

If you're writing about what you got up to at the weekend, on the other hand... well, that probably won't make you much money from AdSense, because what kind of adverts would Google match THAT post to? Adverts for... weekends? As fascinating as that would be, probably not. That's not, of course, to say you shouldn't write those posts: they might work well for your blog in other ways (For instance, those posts might be the ones your regular readers enjoy the most, so they'll keep coming back for them) - but if your aim is to make money from AdSense, you can't ONLY write those posts.

For many new bloggers, myself included, AdSense is an easy introduction to blog monetisation, and for this reason, it's often the first thing people try. Unlike many other ad networks, there's no minimum traffic requirement, so while there are some restrictions on the types of sites that can apply (they'll reject sites that publish pornography, for example, or ones which Google considers to be spam), it's not hard to get accepted, and it's also pretty straightforward to get your ads up and running: simply paste a piece of code into your sidebar, header, or wherever else you've decided to display advertising, and you'll be running ads almost instantly.

What you won't be doing instantly, however, is making much money from those ads. Because AdSense uses a pay-per-click model, you need to have a lot of people clicking on your adverts before you'll make decent money from it: many new bloggers never even reach the minimum payment threshold of $100, and, for this reason, AdSense tends to get a bad rap from bloggers, many of whom claim it's not possible to make good money from it. I have another secret to share with you here, though...

YES, IT IS STILL POSSIBLE TO MAKE MONEY FROM GOOGLE ADSENSE

Up until a couple of years ago, AdSense was my main source of income, and I was making more from it than I used to make from traditional employment. No one ever believes me when I tell them this, because the fact is that while it's certainly possible to make money from AdSense, it's definitely not EASY - and it gets harder with every year that goes by. These days, AdSense is no longer the biggest earner on my blogs, but I do make a reasonable amount of money from it, and there are a couple of reasons for that:

TRAFFIC

Yes, I know I said above that the blog with the most traffic isn't necessarily going to be the biggest AdSense earner, but that doesn't mean you don't need decent traffic from it: you do. One of the reasons no one ever believes me when I say I my blog earns money from AdSense is that most new bloggers who decide to try it out never even make the minimum payout of $100. Why? Because they either don't have enough traffic, they're writing about topics that it's impossible for AdSense to monetise, or because they haven't spent enough time tweaking it. Which brings me to my next "secret":

TWEAKING

Does that sound vaguely rude to anyone else, or is it just me? Actually, just ignore that question...

Another reason many bloggers fail to make any money at all

from AdSense is because they're working on the assumption that it's easy to use: that all you have to do is paste the code into your site, then sit back and watch the money roll in. If it was THAT easy, though, we'd all be AdSense millionaires by now, wouldn't we? The fact is that AdSense IS easy to implement: you literally CAN just paste in the code and have ads up and running in a matter of minutes. You probably won't make much money from those ads, though, because in order to do that, you have to spend a LOT of time tweaking them: by which I mean experimenting with the placement and appearance of your AdSense ads.

There are tons of articles out there which will try to tell you where to place your ads on your blog in order to make the most money. In my case, for instance, I find I get most clicks on adverts which appear at the end of each post, and which use colours which match the rest of my site. That might not be what works best for YOU, though, and I feel like I'm saying this a lot, but to find out what WILL work for you, you have to experiment. One of the biggest AdSense secrets I've ever learned is that this is a method of monetisation in which a small change can make a big difference. Simply changing the colour of the text in your adverts can make your earnings either plummet or skyrocket (OK, mine have never actually "skyrocketed". But you know what I mean.)

Changing the positioning of the adverts, meanwhile... well, that can make or break your earning potential. I once changed my blog theme, and my AdSense earnings dropped to almost nothing overnight... even although this was one of the few templates which my readers almost universally loved, and even although the adverts were in the same place, and used the same basic look, as they had on my previous theme.

You have to spend a LOT of time experimenting, is what I'm trying to say. And if you've spent a lot of time experimenting, and you're STILL not even close to making that minimum payout, you might find you've just learned this secret:

ADSENSE ISN'T FOR EVERYONE

Look, I know I've been kinda signing its praises here, but I don't want to sound like one of those "get rich quick" websites, because the fact is, it's NOT a way to get rich quick - or even slowly, in some cases. As I said above, I've found that AdSense works best on product-based websites, so if your blog isn't one of those, it might never earn you enough money to make it worth using.

I'll also let you into one final secret: it's getting harder and harder to make money from AdSense, to the point where I can see myself stopping using it at some point in the future. Already, my earnings from it are much lower than they were five years ago, say - and that's in spite of the fact that my blog traffic is far higher. There are lots of reasons for this, and I'm going to repeat myself yet again by adding that all-important caveat that I'm speaking purely for myself: but while I don't think you should just dismiss AdSense out of hand, I don't think you should rely on it, either. You need multiple income streams in order to make a sustainable living from blogging: so here's another one for you...

SHOPSTYLE COLLECTIVE

ShopStyle Collective is another pay-per-click scheme, which works in a similar way to AdSense, the main difference being that it isn't contextual: so, rather than simply pasting in a code, and then having ads automatically matched to your site, you have to choose which adverts you'd like to display, and then add them manually. ShopStyle Collective also allows you to add text links to your post which, when clicked on, will generate a few cents of income for you, and there's also a number of different image-based widgets you can try out.

Most of the brands you'll find on ShopStyle are in the fashion and beauty fields, so it obviously works best for bloggers who cover those types of topics. As with Google AdSense, because you're only paid when someone clicks on your link/banner, you'll need a lot of people clicking in order to make money, however it's easy to set up, and can be a good alternative to AdSense.

I've been using ShopSense for around a year now, and it currently earns a little more than AdSense does. Because they're both pay-per-click advertising models, you'll be unsurprised to learn that some of the secrets to making money from them are the same: especially this one...

SHOPSENSE WORKS BEST ON FASHION AND BEAUTY POSTS.

Shopsense is primarily a female-oriented network, which is filled with fashion and beauty brands. Because of this, it works best on... I don't really have to say this, do I? OK, let's state the obvious: it works best on fashion and beauty blogs. Who'da thunk it?

I use Shopsense mostly on my outfit posts, and I'll use a text link to link to the exact items I'm wearing in the photos I've posted, with an image widget underneath, to link to similar items. The idea here is that people read your post, like your outfit, and click on the link to find out where to buy it. Every time they click on a link, you earn a few cents, but here's a secret not a lot of people know:

YOU EARN MORE WHEN PEOPLE ACTUALLY BUY THE PRODUCTS YOU LINK TO.

Although ShopSense is primarily a pay-per-click platform, not everyone will earn the same amount from it. The amount you earn from each click, for instance, will depend on how many of the people who click on your links actually go on to buy the product you linked to. The more sales you make, the higher your "click" amount will be. They don't publicise this much, but if you're not driving sales to the retailers who work with them (i.e. if people are clicking on your links, but not actually buying anything), ShopSense will lower the amount you earn from each click. What this means is that...

YOU REALLY NEED TO MAKE THE ITEMS LOOK ATTRACTIVE.

In order to keep your ShopSense earnings high, you need people to click on your links AND buy the item. For that to happen, you have to really sell the item to them, by showcasing it as best you can. A dark, blurry photograph of you wearing a dress that doesn't fit or flatter you, for instance, isn't going to get anyone reaching for their credit card: this is why the bloggers who earn most from ShopSense, and other affiliate marketing schemes, tend to be the ones who work hardest on creating beautiful images and high-quality content. But! There's one other secret up my sleeve...

SOMETIMES TEXT LINKS CAN EARN THE MOST MONEY.

ShopSense advise you to use image-based links as much as possible, arguing that these are the ones people are most likely to click on. That works in theory, and it sometimes even works in practice. Not ALL the time, though. My own personal experience is that if someone is shown an image of the product, they'll only click on it IF they're seriously thinking of buying it: if they don't want to buy it, they don't NEED to click on that link, because they already KNOW what the product looks like. If they're shown a text link, however, they'll often click on it out of curiosity, which is why text links which require the reader to click on them to find out what you're talking about, will sometimes earn the most money on a site like ShopSense.

You don't, of course, want to abuse this technique: your readers will quickly get annoyed if you're forcing them to constantly click on links, and if they keep on clicking, only to find that the product you linked to is out of their budget anyway, they'll just stop doing it. So use this one sparingly - the goodwill of your readers is worth more than a few cents, anyway.

OTHER FORMS OF AFFILIATE MARKETING

Affiliate marketing is one of the few methods of monetisiation that doesn't necessarily require a huge amount of traffic to work, and, for that reason, it's a method you can use right from the very start, if you want to. I'm not saying you can expect to make a lot of money right from the very start, of course, but hey: every little helps, doesn't it?

The idea behind affiliate marketing is that every time you write about a particular product, you include a link to a website that sells it, and if someone clicks on that link, and then goes on to buy the product in question, you earn commission - normally as a percentage of the sale price. ShopSense is one example of an affiliate marketing network, but there are plenty of others out there. Some brands run their own affiliate schemes, and you'll have to sign up to each one you want to become a member of: others join larger networks, which provide you with lots of different banners and links, all in the same place. Some affiliate networks to check out are:

- Affiliate Window
- Reward Style
- Commission Junction
- Amazon Associates
- Skimlinks

The final option on this list, Skimlinks, is a particularly easy one to try, because Skimlinks will automatically add affiliate links to your content, without any work on your part after the initial installation of it, which simply involves pasting some code into your blog. This list is far from exhaustive, however, so if you're interested in affiliate marketing, hit up Google and see which other networks you can find.

The reason affiliate marketing is a good option for new bloggers is that you genuinely don't need a lot of traffic to your site in order to make money from it. Obviously the more readers you have, the more you'll be able to make, but you only need one person to click on a link/banner and make a purchase, and you'll start earning. Different brands offer different commission levels, but obviously the higher the value of the sale, the more money you make: a small order from low-priced retailer might only make you a few cents, but if someone places a large order from a luxury brand like Net-a-Porter, for instance, your commission will be much higher -

and all from one reader.

I shared quite a few of my affiliate marketing secrets in the section on ShopSense, and most of those tips also apply to the other affiliate networks mentioned here. One thing I didn't mention, however, is that the higher the price of the item, the more commission you'll make when people buy it. For this reason, it's tempting to think you should only ever link to high-value items, which you'll earn the most money from, but you have to consider your audience, too. If most of them can't afford the items you're linking to, you still won't earn commission, so it's a better idea to link to items at a range of different prices, and to show alternatives. (Many bloggers do this by linking to the item they're focusing on, then to a "similar" one, which might be lower priced.) That way if someone does buy that high-value item, you'll make a good commission on it: but if they can't afford it, you'll still have the chance to make something from the lower-priced option.

SPONSORED POSTS

One of the methods of monetising a blog which new bloggers are often most interested in is sponsorship from a brand. This most often takes the form of sponsored posts (where the brand pays the blogger to publish a particular post on their blog), but it could also involve being paid to create an Instagram or other social media post, to provide content for the brand's own website, or to collaborate with the brand in any number of ways. The end result, however, is always the same: the blogger is paid to promote the brand to their audience.

Payments for sponsored posts vary wildly, and will depend on various different factors. There's really only one secret to working with brands, though, and it's this:

BRANDS WORK WITH BLOGGERS
THEY BELIEVE TO BE INFLUENCERS.

A brand will only pay a blogger to collaborate with them if they believe the blogger has the ability to influence people to buy their product or use their service. This is one of those facts that should go without saying, but which apparently doesn't, because I'm constantly seeing new bloggers wonder aloud why X brand won't work with them. A better question, however, would be why SHOULD they? Why would a brand want to pay to appear on your blog (or your social media) unless there was something in it for them? They wouldn't, is the answer to that. It's not the brand's job to send you freebies, or to pay you to write about them: it's the brand's job to sell things, and no matter how friendly they are, and how much they say they love your blog, the truth of the matter is that they will only want to work with you if they think you can help them do that.

How do they know whether you can help them do that?

Good question. Brands measure influence in different ways, but some of the things they might look for are...

TRAFFIC

Ah, THAT again. No matter how awesome your content is, if the only people reading it are your mum and your great Auntie Dot (and to be honest, Dot thinks she's looking at 'The Facebook' most of the time...), there's really not much for a brand to gain by appearing on your blog, is there? Why would they pay to advertise to two people, neither of whom are part of their target market? They won't, is the short answer to that: so if you want brands to work with you, you have to be able to show them that there are enough people reading your blog to make it worth their while.

How many readers are "enough"? Again, this will differ from brand to brand: I know the people who ask me this question are hoping for some sort of target they can aim for ("To work with brands, you need a minimum of 50,000 visitors per month!"), but it just doesn't work like that. Some brands will only work with "top" bloggers, who get hundreds of thousands of visitors per month, others are happy to work with smaller blogs, which they know will still generate plenty of sales for them. You'll know when your blog has reached the stage where brands will want to work with you because... brands will start wanting to work with you. If brands AREN'T yet approaching you with offers of collaborations, you're probably not quite there yet, so stick at it for a while longer.

FOLLOWERS

Another metric brands use to assess whether you're an "influencer" is the number of followers you have: well, I did tell you it was all about the numbers, didn't I? Here, they'll look at how many people follow you on social media, how many subscribe to your RSS feeds, how many have signed up to your email list - that kind of thing. If you don't have many followers, you probably won't get many offers of brand work, either: because why would you, if there's no one listening to what you have to say?

Those aren't the only things brands take into consideration when they're deciding which bloggers they want to collaborate with, obviously: they'll also consider things like the level of engagement you get on your blog and on social media (I.e do people actually comment on your posts and 'like' your Instagram photos, or are they just ...there?), how active you are on the platforms they're interested in promoting themselves on, and various other things besides. While there are tons of different factors a brand MIGHT take into consideration, however, it all boils down to the same thing: they want to know whether or not you'll be able to "sell" them/their product to your readers and followers. So... CAN you?

In order to help you answer this question, I'm going to turn it on its head slightly. The thing I hear most often from new bloggers, you see, isn't "What can I do for this brand?" (which is what the brand themselves will be asking), but "Why isn't this brand working with me?" So let's take a look at that, shall we?

WHY BRANDS AREN'T WORKING WITH YOUR BLOG

1. YOU'RE NOT BIG ENOUGH

Hard to hear, yes, but important to accept: no one is going to be falling over themselves to work with a brand-new blogger, who only has 15 followers, and who doesn't have any real influence over any of them yet. Sucks, doesn't it? Don't beat yourself up over this, obviously: the fact that you don't have a huge amount of traffic or followers yet doesn't mean your blog is bad, or that you won't ever get there - it just means you're not there YET. There's absolutely nothing wrong with starting a blog with the primary aim of making money from it, but it's a mistake to assume that anyone owes you a living, and that you're going to instantly start pulling in sponsorships: you're just not. You're going to need traffic and followers first, and that means you're going to need time. So give yourself some.

2. YOU HAVE A CRAPPY LOOKING BLOG

Blog readers are complex creatures: they like lots of different things, and some of them actively prefer (or at least CLAIM to prefer) blogs which have a bit of an "amateurish" look to them, because they believe them to be more "authentic". (There's a lot I could say about THAT particular idea, by the way, but I'm going to refrain...) Brands, on the other hand, are a lot simpler, and much easier to understand. They're not ALL like this, of course, but for the most part, brands value professionalism: they want to be associated with blogs that are shiny, and glossy, and which look like the blogger has taken some care over them. I'm not saying here that they're RIGHT to feel like that, and I'm certainly not saying that blogs with slick designs and professional-looking graphics are better than ones which look like they've been thrown together on their author's lunch break, but the fact is, if you want your blog to be a business, you're going to have to drop the "never judge a book by a cover" attitude. Your book IS going to be judged by its cover, unfortunately: so make sure it's a good one.

3. YOU TAKE TERRIBLE PHOTOS

So you can't afford a decent camera/ don't have a "blogger boyfriend" to follow you around taking endless photos of you / you work all day, and don't get home until it's pitch dark outside, etc etc. Look, that's pretty rough, seriously: it'll make it REALLY hard for you to get decent photos for your blog, and that's a real shame. It's also something you're going to have to try your best to overcome if you want to work with brands, however, because brands don't want to pay people to take terrible photos of their products. Well, D'UH! If YOU had a product to sell, would YOU pay someone to lay it out on their rumpled duvet cover, and take a blurry photo of it at midnight, with next to no lighting, and no way to really see what the hell it is you're supposed to be looking at? I doubt it.

Brands are the same way. This is such an obvious fact, but it's one that a lot of bloggers really struggle to understand. The thing is, most people just don't want to hear any of this. When they ask me how to get brands to sponsor them, they want me to say there's not much to it: that of COURSE brands will want to work with their 2-week old blog, with the generic Blogspot template and the mirror selfies in which you can't actually see what they're wearing. They want me to say brands don't care about "the numbers": they're able to see beyond that, and appreciate the true passion the blogger has for their subject. And brands don't want bloggers to do magazine-style photo shoots! Of COURSE not! They LIKE the mirror selfies! They find them charmingly authentic, and that's exactly what they're after, isn't it?

Newsflash: no, it isn't. It really isn't. When a brand decides to work with a blogger, they want the blogger to do the best job possible of selling their product. They want them to take fabulous photos, in which the product appears to its absolute best advantage. They want those photos to appear on a professional-looking blog, which thousands of people read, and are influenced by. They want that, because THAT'S what sells products: and that's what you're ultimately doing here, isn't it? Don't let yourself be fooled into thinking the brand is just being "friendly", or is offering to send you a free dress out of the kindness of their hearts, or to "reward" you for your loyal custom. They're not. They're sending you it because they want you to sell it for them: and you're probably not going to do that with a mirror selfie, are you?

That was all pretty negative, wasn't it? Sorry about that. Let's say you didn't need any of that advice, then: let's say you have an awesome, professional-looking blog, filled with fabulous photos, and followed by thousands of highly-engaged followers. How do you go about getting brands to work with you?

The short answer to this question is that if you have all of that, you probably won't have to do ANYTHING to get brands to notice you: they already will, and THEY'LL be the ones to approach YOU. I'll let you into a personal secret:

I don't do anything at all to get brands to sponsor me.

Actually, wait: that's not quite true. I do my very best, every single day, to create quality content, that people will want to read. I do that because I know that's what makes blogs successful, and successful blogs are the ones brands want to work with. OTHER than that, though, I do absolutely nothing: I don't go out and actively pursue collaborations, and I've never contacted a brand asking them to sponsor me in my life: they've always come to me.

Now, before you start rolling your eyes at me, I'm not saying this is the best way to proceed, because if you're running your blog as a business, it's just silly to sit back and wait for clients to find you, isn't it? When I started blogging, however, I was absolutely clueless: it didn't even occur to me that people might want to pay me to feature on my blog, so when the offers started trickling in, I was pretty blown away by it.

These days, I have an agency who deals with collaborations for me. How did I get signed by an agency? By building my blog to the point where it was getting enough traffic for agencies to be interested in working with me. Probably not the answer you were hoping for, but no matter what your question is*, the answer is almost ALWAYS going to be "Work on making your blog the best it can possibly be." That's just the way it works.

(*Unless your question is, "How much is that doggie in the window?" or "Do you know the way to San Jose?" or something: THOSE questions will have really quite different answers...)

So, my agency deals with the brands who approach them looking to work with bloggers, and that works for me, because - another secret coming up - the fact is, I don't actually LIKE doing collaborations all that much. Don't get me wrong: I'm grateful for them and they help pay the bills, but I'd much rather be left to my own devices, writing about only the topics I WANT to write about, as opposed the ones that are chosen for me by sponsors. Because of that, I'm content to do only those sponsored posts that are offered to me: that's a personal choice I've made, and I know that I'd probably be making much more money if I was actively pursuing opportunities myself.

So, how do you do THAT?

The first way you do it is by having an awesome blog that everyone is talking about: if you have that, you can basically just sit back and wait for the offers to come rolling in, because when everyone's heard of you and your blog, those brands you want to work with just won't be able to avoid hearing about you, right?

Well, yes, BUT... we all know that's not so easy, don't we? There are a lot of great blogs out there, so if brands aren't singling yours out fast enough, your next option is to reach out to them yourself. You can do that the old-fashioned way, by emailing them (or even the REALLY old-fashioned way, by phoning them. Hey, remember that? It's what people did before texting was invented?), or the more subtle method of reaching out to them on social media.

One easy way to get a brand to notice you is by writing about them on your blog, and then tagging them on your social media: so, if you're a fashion blogger, say, you create a blog post in which you're wearing an item from Brand X, and then promote it on Twitter and Instagram by saying something like, "Here's my latest post, in which I'm wearing a dress by @BrandX!" The theory is that Brand X will see this, and think, "Hey, this blogger seems awesome: let's work with her!" Sometimes this will work, and sometimes it won't, which is why your final option if you want to work with brands is to sign up to an agency or website designed to help you do exactly that.

The downside to this, of course, is that no agency is going to do this for free: they'll charge a commission (normally a percentage of your fee), and it's up to you to decide whether you think it's worth going down this route. If you do, some agencies which aim to connect bloggers with advertisers include:

- IZEA.com
- handpickedmedia.co.uk
- thebloggerprogramme.com
- SocialFabric.us
- Whoispollinate.com
- CleverGirlsCollective.com
- Linquia.com

This short list is just a starting point: do a quick Google search you'll find tons of different agencies out there who'll help you find sponsored posts - or try to, anyway. Bear in mind that each agency will have different terms and conditions, and that the ones above are not all ones I've tried personally, so make sure you read their sites carefully, and know what you're getting in to.

And that's how you make money from blogging! Simple, huh?

This list is, of course, not exhaustive: there are many, many different ways to monetise a blog, and as the industry is in such a constant state of change, new methods are popping up all the time. These options are the ones I use personally, however, and they're also some of the most common ways of making money from blogging: so keep experimenting, keep working hard, and you'll find the option that works best for you.

AMBER McNAUGHT

9

HOW I GREW MY BLOG TO OVER 180,000 PAGE VIEWS PER MONTH

So, you've read this far (Or, at least, I HOPE you've read this far, or I've given myself RSI for nothing...), but if you're anything like me, I'm guessing you probably still have questions, don't you? And I'm guessing the biggest one is this:

What next?

I mean, you know how to start a blog, how to create content for a blog, and how to make money from a blog. But let's face facts: lots of people know those things, don't they? There are thousands and thousands of blogs out there, and some of them are really good ones, too, but not all of them are actually making money, are they? Even fewer are making a living, and hardly any are making a fortune... so what's the REAL secret of successful blogging? That's what you really want to know, isn't it? Because there has to be one, doesn't there? There has to be a reason why some blogs are successful and others aren't - even although the ones that aren't seem to be doing all the right things, and diligently following all of the so-called "rules".

When you've worked your butt off to create a blog you're proud of, and you're still not getting the results you want from it, it's really easy to become despondent, and to assume there's something you're missing. The fact is, though, it's totally possible to do everything right and STILL not see your blog take off the way you want it to. It happened to me: quite a few times, actually. The truth is, my blog has been online for a decade now... but it's only really been what I'd call "successful" for the last few years. Up until then, it just kind of... existed. Oh, don't get me wrong: I had readers. I even had a few sponsors, and advertisers - and, what's more, I had some really awesome feedback, too. The people who read my blog told me they loved it. The people who advertised told me they were thrilled with the results. I had a small, but highly-engaged audience, and I was creating content I was proud of...

... but I still wasn't making money.

Or not enough of it, anyway. Yes, my blog made SOME money: but not enough for me to live off. In fact, up until a couple of years ago, in order to be able to work from home, and earn a living from blogging, I was having to run three blogs: Forever Amber, ShoeperWoman.com and TheFashionPolice.net. None of the three was what you'd call hugely successful on its own, but between them, they pulled in a fairly respectable income, and for years I worked on the assumption that if I wanted to continue to make a living from blogging, I'd have to continue to run multiple websites. There was just one problem with that:

I really hated having to run multiple websites.

I mean, don't get me wrong: I didn't hate it in that "crying in the shower" way I'd hated every other job I'd ever had - far from it. I enjoyed writing for each of my blogs: what I didn't enjoy was having to split my time between them all - to take all of the different tasks a blogger has to do every day, and then to multiply them by three... and to basically keep doing that forever.

It was stressful. It was dull. And, more importantly, it wasn't really working. The fact is, when you try to split your attention between three different blogs, none of them gets the attention it needs to really thrive. I was doing OK financially, but I was constantly left feeling like I wasn't doing my best work, and that while each of my blogs was doing just fine, I'd be happier if just one of them could do MORE than fine. Something had to change, and that something was my mindset. I can tell you exactly when that change happened, too:

It was the 13th of June, 2014.

Yeah, I really wasn't joking when I used the word "exactly".

How on earth do I know this? I know because I wrote about it on my blog: not about the change in mindset, but about the day itself. It was a beautiful, sunny day, you see, and my husband Terry and I decided we'd take the day off and head into Edinburgh, to the Botanical Gardens there. I say "take the day off": because we're both self-employed (Terry still does web design), we're able to arrange our schedules however we like, so on this particular day, we decided to spend the day out enjoying the sunshine (we don't get a lot of it in Scotland, so we have to make the most of it while we can...), and the evening catching up with work.

It really was a beautiful day, and I was thoroughly enjoying wandering around the beautiful gardens, but there was a nagging undercurrent of guilt. The whole time we were relaxing in the sunshine, I knew the work was piling up at home, and I'd probably have to be up until late, doing all of the various tasks I needed to do to keep my three blogs running. Wouldn't it be awesome, I thought, if I only had ONE site to run, and if that one site was Forever Amber, my lifestyle blog? One blog still requires a lot of work, obviously, but if the blog in question was the one which centred around writing about my life, then this day out I was currently enjoying wouldn't be "time off" - it would be all part of the job. We had, after all, brought the camera along, so I could take some outfit photos for Forever Amber. If I didn't have the other two sites to worry about, I'd be able to go home, write up the post (which didn't feel like work to me, the way writing for the other two sites did), and be done for the day.

I knew it wouldn't be like that ALL the time, obviously: I couldn't expect to just have days out all the time, write about them, and earn enough from that to live on. But having just one blog would drastically reduce my stress levels, and would also allow me to focus all of my time and energy on making that blog as good as it could possibly be.

So that's what I decided to do.

It's important to note here that I didn't just drop the other two blogs: I couldn't afford to, as those were the sites that were making the most money back then. At the time of writing, I still have them both, but they're really just a safety net, more than anything else. I can't quite bring myself to let them go entirely, but since that day in 2013, I've drastically changed the way I operate them. The Fashion Police now gets just one post per week, and ShoeperWoman had a complete change in direction, to make it much easier for me to keep it running. I now spend the minimum amount of time possible on those two sites, while the majority of my time is spent on Forever Amber: the blog that started out as a personal diary, and which is now a thriving business. In less than three years, I'd taken

Forever Amber from being the smallest of my blogs, to by far the largest. I'd more than doubled the traffic it received, and turned it into the biggest earner of all of my blogs, and my main source of income.

Here's how I did it...

THE SECRETS OF MY BLOG'S GROWTH

After reading what I've said above, you're probably thinking one of two things. You're either thinking, "Wow, great: it's possible to turn your blog into a business in just under three years!" or - and this is probably more likely - you're thinking:

"Wait: THREE YEARS? Isn't that kind of a long time to wait?"

Well, it is and it isn't. If you were paying attention at the start of this book (and I hope you were, because there'll be a quiz at the end...), you might recall all of those words of caution I threw at you: all that stuff about how blogging isn't easy, and it takes time and effort to build a successful blog.

Er, I really wasn't joking about any of that stuff: it's all true. This isn't some kind of "get rich quick" scheme you're buying into here: it's a business, and most businesses don't achieve overnight success. Some do, of course - and some blogs do, too. Some people actually DO start a blog, and achieve almost instant success with it: the problem is that because those blogs become so well-known, people tend to think that their experience is the norm, when it's actually an anomaly (and down to pure luck, in many cases). Most successful blogs don't achieve success overnight - or even over the course of a few months, so if that's what you're expecting, you better hope you're going to be one of the lucky ones.

I WASN'T one of the lucky ones, as you can tell. I was one of the ones who had to work hard, for a long time, without seeing much in the way of a result. In fact, for the first five years of my blog's life, I saw very little growth at all: the traffic graph on my Google Analytics account was pretty much a straight line, and nothing I did seemed to make it change.

In other words, I'm the living proof that it's totally possible to blog for years on end without ever becoming successful.

So, what happened in June 2013 to cause my traffic to increase, all of a sudden? It can't have been JUST the fact that I decided to spend more time on the site... could it?

Actually, yes, it could. That sudden increase in traffic was totally down to the fact that in June 2013, I decided to stop treating my blog as a hobby that also earned me some money (or as just one, relatively unimportant, part of a much larger business, rather), and start treating it as a business in its own right. Having that mindset is a huge change in itself, and a really important one, too. One of the things I notice most about many of the bloggers who ask me for advice is that they aren't treating their blogs as businesses: often because they either don't think they "deserve" that title ("Oh, but this is just a little project I do in my spare time!"), or because they've yet to shake off the idea that blogging should only ever be a hobby, and that they should be able to essentially just make money from treating it as such.

I blogged that way for years, though - as if it was simply a hobby. I wrote what I wanted, when I wanted to, and I didn't give money a second thought - which meant I didn't actually make any of it. For YEARS.

In 2013, however, I decided to start taking my blog more seriously: to treat it more like a business, and to make business decisions (rather than purely personal ones) relating to it. As soon as I started to do that, my traffic and revenue started to increase: here are some of the things I did that helped make that happen...

1. I started posting more frequently

At the point I decided to get serious about my blogging business, I was posting roughly three times per week, although that wasn't set in stone. I always aimed to have a new post up on Mondays, Wednesdays and Fridays, but it didn't always happen: some weeks I'd only manage one posts, and other weeks I'd have no new content to post at all.

Now, I talked in an earlier chapter about how the ideal posting schedule is simply the one that works best for you and your blog, and how there's no "right" answer to the question of how often you should post: quality will always be more important than quantity, and I stand by that observation. Having said that, though, there's no getting away from the fact that the more frequently you can post new content - WITHOUT compromising the quality- the more traffic your blog will be likely to get. More content means more opportunities for people to click a link on social media, more pages to be indexed by Google (and to hopefully show up in their search), and more posts to be linked from other blogs. It also means your regular readers will be visiting your blog multiple times each week, rather than just once or twice, and that will, in turn, increase your pageviews. All the good things, basically.

In my case, the reason I'd been posting infrequently had nothing to do with my content. It wasn't that I had nothing to write about, or that I didn't know how to go about it: it was purely because I wasn't making time for it. My blog wasn't my priority: I viewed it as "just a hobby", so updating it was always the last thing on my "to do" list, and the first thing to be bumped if I was having a particularly busy week. Can you imagine a coffee shop owner, say, who only opened up when he felt like it, or when he had nothing better to do? Of course not: because businesses don't work that way, and blogs don't either.

When I decided I wanted to turn my hobby blog into a business, the first thing I did was to make my blog my number one priority - after family and health, obviously. That meant making time to create content, sticking to a schedule, and generally moving all things blog to the top of the 'to do' list, rather than the bottom.

Many bloggers sneer at this kind of thing. They resent the idea of having to generate more content, and they particularly resent the idea of having to blog to a schedule, feeling that it kills the spontaneity of writing. The first thing I'll say here is that your schedule doesn't have to be a rigid one (no one's really going to notice if you don't have a new post up at 9am on the dot, or if you miss a day or two here and there), and you don't have to blog every day, either, if that doesn't work for you. You can still have your spontaneity: but there's no doubt in my mind that consistency is one of the keys to my blog's success - and that posting more content got me more readers.

2. I experimented with different types of content

For the first few years of its life, my blog was strictly a personal diary, and I stuck rigidly to that format. I didn't do outfit posts, because it wasn't a fashion blog, and I didn't do product reviews because it wasn't a beauty blog - so even although I was really interested in both of those subjects, I actively avoided writing about them, because I worried that my readers would be annoyed by the change in content. Crazy, huh?

Eventually, though, I came to realise that writing about only those things my readers DID expect me to write about wasn't actually getting me anywhere. Sure, it was keeping my small group of regular readers happy, but it wasn't increasing my readership, or helping my blog grow. They say the definition of insanity is doing the same thing over and over again, and expecting different results, but that's exactly what I was doing. I was writing the same type of content, in the same way - and, of course, it was being read by exactly the same readers.

Not long before the Great Change of June 2013, I started to include outfit posts on my blog, along with the other content. Almost immediately, my traffic started to increase, as the blog was discovered by a whole new readership... and then the growth stalled again. Luckily by this time I'd learned my lesson: I knew I couldn't just keep on doing the same old thing, and expect my blog to grow, so I continued to experiment with the topics I was I writing about, and the style of post I was creating.

Probably the biggest change here was the introduction of that "evergreen" content I talked about earlier in this book. Up until then, almost all of my posts had been the "time sensitive" type. Diary style posts are only really relevant when they're first published, after all (no one really cares about what a random blogger got up to last year, do they?), and even outfit posts will date quickly - the clothes are no longer available, the seasons change, the post stops getting traffic, and is all but forgotten.

I continued writing those posts, of course - because while they might not have had a long shelf life, they WERE popular at the time they were published - but I also started to supplement them with that "evergreen" content I've talked so much about. Tutorials. 'How Tos'. Anything that was potentially helpful to someone, or which they might conceivably search Google for. And THAT was when my blog finally started to grow. Between June 2013 and now, the traffic graph shows a steady upwards climb: sure, there have been times when it's leveled out for a while, and even times when it's dipped, but for the most part, it's an upward trend, and that continued growth is a direct result of me deciding to take my blog more seriously, to start treating it as a business, rather than as a hobby, and to stop just doing the same old things, and yet expecting different results. Here are some more specific things I attribute my blog's growth to:

3. I told my story

My blog started out as a personal journal, so you could say that I've been telling my story from the moment I started it, and I credit that as one of the main reasons for its early success.

Now, I'm not saying here that your blog should basically be a very long autobiography, and even if it is, it definitely shouldn't be the "tell all" kind. You really can't tell the WHOLE story - and if you try to, well, that could be a really good way to get yourself sued by someone who doesn't want to be written about on the internet, or to just really put people off with the obscene level of over-sharing you'd be indulging in.

What I'm suggesting instead, however, is that you really think long and hard about your story, and how you want to tell it. What is it that makes you YOU? What experiences do you have to share? What I realised from writing some of the more personal posts on my blog is that people are fundamentally interested in... other people. Sure, they might come to my blog because they're initially interested in fashion, or beauty, or whichever topic it was that they typed into Google to find me, but they'll stay because they're interested in my story - and the readers who are there for your story are the most loyal of all.

A lot of bloggers don't bother to tell their story. They decide they're going to be fashion bloggers, or beauty bloggers, say, so they post outfit photos and product reviews, and they don't stop to ask themselves why anyone should care about what they're wearing, or what their opinion was of that lipstick. That sounds harsh, but think about it: unless your outfits are very unique, and exceptionally awesome (and if they are, you probably don't need any of my advice), no one really cares about what you're wearing every day, do they? In order for people to be interested in what you're wearing, you have to first of all interest them in YOU - and you do that by telling them your story.

Or that's what I did, anyway. There are tons of bloggers out there who don't give any insight into themselves or their lives: they just seem to prance around all day, looking like they stepped out of a Vogue shoot, and people follow them because they're so impressed by their style that they want to copy it. I'm not one of those people, though, and if you're not one either, you have to think long and hard about what else you can bring to the party other than photos of your outfits or product reviews you could just as easily find on Amazon.

I'll be honest: I DO have some readers who follow me purely for the outfits - I know because they've told me. "I'm not interested in your life," wrote one particularly harsh commenter. "I just want to see your shoes." There are readers who are like that, sure. It's a mistake to write for those people, though, because the fact is that the girl who's only interested in my shoes will only read my blog as long as I continue to wear nice shoes, and that's a hard role to live up to. What if my taste in shoes changes, for instance? What if I sprain my ankle and can't wear heels anymore? Do I have to keep on wearing clothes I don't like, or can't actually walk in, just to keep this reader happy? Well, yes, actually: that IS what I'd have to do. I don't do that, though, because I know there's no pleasing people who are only interested in one tiny detail of my blog: they'll stop reading as soon as they lose interest in that thing - and they WILL lose interest in it, sooner or later.

The reader who's interested in the story I have to tell while wearing those shoes, though? That reader will be in it for the long haul - and that's exactly the kind of reader I need.

4. I didn't just write "for myself".

One of the pieces of advice people like to give bloggers is that you should write, first and foremost, "for yourself."

I don't do that.

That, after all, is what personal journals are for: and trust me - if I were to write purely "for myself", without any thought as to what might actually be of interest to other people, I can guarantee that no one would want to read it. I know, because I've done it: I kept a "personal diary" style blog for years without seeing any growth at all, and it wasn't until I started to ask myself what other people could possibly get out of my blog, and to adapt the content accordingly, that it finally started to grow.

Of course, sometimes all those "other people" are looking for from your blog is entertainment. If you've followed the advice above, and made your blog personal in some way, your readers will hopefully have started to feel like they know you a little - and when your readers feel like they know you, not only will they find it easier to trust you, they'll hopefully be interested in what you have to say about whichever topic you've chosen to blog about.

As for newer readers, however - well, that's a little trickier, and the fact is that brand new visitors to your blog won't care about what you have to say unless you give them a reason to. In my case, I do this by mixing my personal posts with useful, evergreen content, which will both bring new readers to the site, and give them a reason to follow it. So, rather than simply doing a "Here's what I wore today" post, you might consider doing a "How to wear..." one instead, for instance. Rather than a straightforward product review, you could do something along the lines of "three products that are perfect for pale skin" - and so on. Not all of your content has to be useful, obviously - but if you're only writing posts about yourself, without asking what other people might get out of reading them, you might find it harder to grow your readership.

5. I wasn't afraid to write long posts

Another piece of bad blogging advice that people are fond of giving out is that you shouldn't write long blog posts. "People don't read them!" the bloggers who give this advice proclaim. "You have to make sure your posts are short and to the point, or they'll never be read!"

Now, there's absolutely nothing wrong with writing short, concise blog posts, IF that's your style. It's not mine, though. My posts tend to be long - sometimes VERY long - and my experience is that the length of my posts has only ever benefited my blog. My very longest posts, for instance, are amongst some of the most popular, and I regularly get comments from readers saying they really enjoy being able to settle down and read something a bit longer, and more in-depth than your standard 300-word blog post.

Of course, some readers complain about the length, too - you can't please everyone, and I said in the chapter on content creation, the only thing you have to understand here is that there is no "ideal" length for a blog post. It's certainly true that longer posts give search engines more content to index, and are often seen as more "authoritative" (Well, it's hard to look like an expert on something when you can't come up with more than 100 words to say about it, isn't it?), but it's also true that waffling on for a few hundred words, purely for the sake of filling space, won't really do your blog any favours either.

Remember: your blog post should be exactly as long as it needs to be for you to tell your story or get your point across. That's all you need to know.

6. I started to pay as much attention to photography as I did to writing

I hate looking back at the earliest posts on my blog: most of them have no images whatsoever (which makes them look very dry, now that I'm used to today's style of all-singing, all-dancing websites), and the ones that DO have images make me cringe in horror at how very, very bad those images are. Back then, though, I figured I didn't need to worry about photos, because the writing was the most important part - and and back then, it was. That was then, though. These days, blogs have changed: they're slicker, glossier, and, most importantly, the ones that are really successful all have at least one thing in common - great photography.

It stands to reason that if you're a fashion blogger, or your field of interest is similarly visual, that you'll have to illustrate your posts with images of some kind: well, it wouldn't be quite the same if you were to just describe what you're wearing, rather than taking a photo of it, would it? Photography doesn't come easy to me - in fact, it's the part of the job I like least - but investing a little bit of time and money in improving my skills in that area has really paid off.

7. I tried my best to be consistent

Consistency is absolutely crucial when it comes to running a blog business, and in the early days of my own blogging career, I'd say it was the main reason I managed to gain some followers. Blog readers are creatures of habit: they tend to read the blogs they like at a certain time (maybe over their morning coffee, say, or during the commute to work), and because of that, they like to know what to expect, and when to expect it. I'm not saying you have to be absolutely rigid about this, and stick to a particular schedule, no matter what, but if you don't keep producing new content for people to read, you can't claim to be too surprised when they stop visiting your blog, can you?

Oh, and when I talk about consistency, I'm not just referring to the quantity of posts you manage to crank out every week - I'm also talking about the quality. Keep it high, don't fall into the trap of publishing posts you're not proud of just because you feel like you have to write SOMETHING, and pay attention to your spelling and grammar - because yes, it matters.

8. I turned down more collaborations than I accepted

Once your blog starts to gain traction, you'll start to receive emails from brands looking to collaborate. Most of these brands will be out to get something for nothing - or as close to nothing as they can get, anyway - so they'll normally offer to send you a product in exchange for a "review". When you're new to blogging, it's hard to say no to this kind of thing: you're normally so flattered that someone noticed your blog and wanted to collaborate with you that you're more than happy to accept the "free stuff" they're offering to send you (Well, everyone likes FREE STUFF, right?), and then, because you're you, and you care about the quality of the content you put onto your blog, you'll spend hours photographing it, writing about it and promoting it. It's only when you've done this a half dozen times or more that the penny will drop, and you'll be all, "Wait: did I really just work for five hours in exchange for a tube of toothpaste?"

The fact is - and I really can't emphasize this enough - a

product isn't "free" if you have to work for it. The brands who contact you with these offers aren't just doing it out of the kindness of their hearts: they expect something in return, so when they say "review", they mean "it better be a good one", and when they say "gift" they mean, "If you don't have a post up the day after it arrives, we'll hound you relentlessly until you do." This isn't a great deal for you as a blogger: there's an obvious benefit to brands in being featured on a popular blog, but there's really not much in it for the blogger - which is why most of those who blog for a living will expect to be paid for the collaborations they take part in.

At first, that might sound a bit greedy: it did to me. I spent years happily accepting "free" dresses and shoes in exchange for blog posts which would take me hours and hours to write. And you know what? I might have ended up with a bulging closet, but my bank account was anything but, because it turns out the bank doesn't accept clothes and shoes as payments towards your mortgage. The supermarket doesn't accept them either, and nor does any other retailer I've ever encountered: so if you're still thinking it's greedy to accept the free clothes AND expect to be paid to wear them (I mean, THE CHEEK!), you might want to ask yourself how you're planning to pay your bills if all you have to show for your hard work is a closet full of dresses. (Which, OK, is a pretty cool thing to have, let's be honest.)

These days, I no longer accept products in exchange for coverage on my blog. Sure, I might say yes to the odd dress or two, if it's something I REALLY love, but for the most part, I expect to paid for the work I do, just like anyone else. I'm also extremely picky about the brands I'll collaborate with. I mean, I run a fashion and lifestyle blog, which mostly centres around vintage-inspired fashion, and I once received a request to blog about men's workboots - the kind with the steel toecaps and clunky shape. Now, you couldn't pay me to wear those boots, and I mean that literally, because they DID offer to pay me, and I said no. Because if I'd accepted that collaboration, I'd have made some money, but I'd have lost the respect of my readers, who know perfectly well I wouldn't ever wear men's workboots: so, in the long run, I'd lose.

I wish I could say that was the strangest collaboration request I've ever had, but every single week I get an offer that makes me scratch my head and think, "Has this person even SEEN my blog?" because what they're asking me to write about is just so far removed from my usual style/content that saying "yes" to it wouldn't do either of us any good. (My "favourite" one was for incontinence products. Yes, really.) So I say "no", instead, and doing that gives me time to work on content that WILL benefit my blog. Remember what I said about consistency? If you want to be consistent, you have to fiercely protect your content: don't let it be diluted with tons of irrelevant collaborations, or compromised by content that just isn't the right fit.

9. I concentrated my efforts on the social networks that worked best for me.

I'm not a big fan of social media, but because it drives so much traffic to my blog every day, it would be pretty silly of me to ignore it altogether. Trying to be equally active on every single social network out there, however, would mean spreading myself so thin I'd have no time to blog: instead, I choose to focus solely on the networks that work best for me (Pinterest and Instagram), and use Wordpress plugins to automatically promote my posts on all the rest. I know I could grow my blog faster if I paid more attention to the networks I'm currently neglecting, but, well, there's only one of me, and working round the clock just to remain active on social media wouldn't actually help my blog in the long run, would it?

Want to know one of the biggest secrets of my blogging success, though?

10. I didn't quit.

Many bloggers DO quit. They start a blog because it seems like a cool thing to do, and then, as soon as they realise how much work goes into running it (and how long you have to wait before you see any return on that time investment), they give up, defeated.

Me? I never gave up, and that's one of the main reasons I'm still blogging, ten years later. You wouldn't give up your "real" job just because it was hard, after all, and you can't afford to give up on blogging either, if you're truly serious about making a living from it. Instead, you have to keep at it: keep learning, keep evolving, and, above all, KEEP BLOGGING. Yes, even when you think no one is reading - or maybe ESPECIALLY when you think no one is reading.

Successful blogging is a constant learning process. It's not enough to find a formula that works for you, and to assume it will work forever - because one day it might not, and then where will you be? Because online publishing is still a relatively new industry, it's changing constantly: blogging today is not the same as it was a couple of years ago, and it's not the same as it will be a few years from now. So, as well as continuing to create great content on a regular schedule, you'll also have to try your best to stay ahead of the curve: to pay attention to those changes, and to try to make them work for you, rather than against you.

The good news is that if you can do that, you'll be making a living doing something you love: because blogging is the kind of job you HAVE to love, if you want to make it a career. If you don't love it, you'll find it hard to sacrifice the long hours and complete change of lifestyle that's required to sustain it: and the lack of financial security might not seem like enough of a reward if you don't really love what you do.

So, as I said back at the start of this book, if you want to quit your job and blog for a living, it helps if you hate your job: and are prepared to do just about anything to change it.

If you enjoyed this book, please visit my blog,

www.ForeverAmber.co.uk,

where you'll find more blog tips and advice.

forever Amber